CBT Toolbox for Children and Teens

202 Engaging Activities and Exercises for Kids and Adolescents to Successfully Manage Emotions, Conquer Worries, and Foster Positive Habits

© Copyright 2023 - All rights reserved.

The content contained within this book may not be reproduced, duplicated, or transmitted without direct written permission from the author or the publisher.

Under no circumstances will any blame or legal responsibility be held against the publisher or author for any damages, reparation, or monetary loss due to the information contained within this book, either directly or indirectly.

Legal Notice:

This book is copyright-protected. It is only for personal use. You cannot amend, distribute, sell, use, quote, or paraphrase any part of the content within this book without the consent of the author or publisher.

Disclaimer Notice:

Please note the information contained within this document is for educational and entertainment purposes only. All effort has been executed to present accurate, up-to-date, reliable, and complete information. No warranties of any kind are declared or implied. Readers acknowledge that the author is not engaging in the rendering of legal, financial, medical, or professional advice. The content within this book has been derived from various sources. Please consult a licensed professional before attempting any techniques outlined in this book.

By reading this document, the reader agrees that under no circumstances is the author responsible for any losses, direct or indirect, that are incurred as a result of the use of the information contained within this document, including, but not limited to, errors, omissions, or inaccuracies.

Table of Contents

PART 1: CBT TOOLBOX FOR KIDS 1
    INTRODUCTION LETTER TO PARENTS 2
    INTRODUCTION LETTER TO CHILDREN 3
    SECTION 1: WHAT AM I FEELING? 4
    SECTION 2: EXPRESSING MYSELF 22
    SECTION 3: TAMING MY FEARS 32
    SECTION 4: PUTTING MY ANGER TO SLEEP 41
    SECTION 5: KEEPING MY WORRIES AWAY 47
    SECTION 6: ANXIETY FIGHTERS 53
    SECTION 7: MY ZEN ZONE 62
    SECTION 8: HEALTHY HABITS, HAPPY MINDS 67
    SECTION 9: CONQUERING MY BIGGEST CHALLENGES 73
    SECTION 10: EMBRACING MYSELF 80
    BONUS SECTION: THOUGHT CHALLENGE 87
    THANK YOU 89
PART 2: CBT TOOLBOX FOR TEENS 90
    LETTER TO THE PARENT 91
    LETTER TO THE TEENAGER 93
    SECTION 1: HOW CAN CBT HELP ME? 94
    SECTION 2: THOUGHTS, EMOTIONS, AND BEHAVIORS 104
    SECTION 3: TAMING ANXIETY 114
    SECTION 4: FACING MY FEAR 121
    SECTION 5: OVERCOMING MENTAL FILTERING 133
    SECTION 6: BEATING THE BLUES 143
    SECTION 7: CONTROLLING ANGER 153
    SECTION 8: MY SELF-ESTEEM 164
    SECTION 9: NO MORE "SHOULDS" 183

SECTION 10: PEACE WITHIN YOU 190
BONUS SECTION: MY BEHAVIOR LOG 197
THANK YOU 199
CHECK OUT ANOTHER BOOK IN THE SERIES 200
REFERENCES 201

Part 1: CBT Toolbox for Kids

101 Fun Activities and Exercises to Help Children Deal with Difficult Emotions, Conquer Worries, and Develop Healthy Habits

Introduction Letter to Parents

Dear Parents,

This book is a comprehensive CBT toolbox for children. CBT stands for Cognitive Behavioral Therapy, a therapeutic protocol that helps with various problems, including anxiety and depression. The tools outlined in the exercises will equip your child with the skills needed to form strong relationships, solve problems, and regulate their emotions.

By working through these exercises, your child will be given skills that can be applied throughout their life. The CBT activities are structured in such a way as to incorporate mental, physical, and emotional well-being. Many adults do not know how to work through their emotions and traumatic experiences. This lack of understanding of their minds can lead to adverse outcomes. Your desire to protect your child is admirable, but you cannot be there all the time. Therefore, the exercises here are created in a way that lays the foundation for independence and helps instill critical thinking and emotional intelligence, which are needed to navigate a volatile world.

Introduction Letter to Children

Dear Children,

Sometimes, life can get tough and be very confusing. You will experience moments when the confusion of life causes you to be angry, annoyed, frustrated, and unhappy. This book gives you the tools you need to make positive changes to help you feel better about yourself and your relationships with your friends and family.

There is a lot that happens in the world that you cannot control. You must learn to accept what you can and cannot control. One of the things you have control over is your mind. This book teaches you how your mind works and how you can use your mind to become a better person and achieve all your dreams. By completing all these exercises, you will realize how much potential you have and how much you can change the world just by being yourself.

Section 1: What Am I Feeling?

Do you know what feelings are?

When you are having fun with your friends, you will feel happy. If you get into an argument with one of your classmates, you will feel angry.

Feelings are all the different ways that people can feel on the inside. People feel good when things they like happen, and they feel bad when things do not go their way.

Another word for feelings is emotions. Your emotions change all the time during the day. Some emotions stay around longer than others.

Notebook or Copybook Journal

Before you begin, ask your parents for a notebook or a copybook journal. This book will help you do many of the exercises in this book. Enjoy!

Exercise 1

Sometimes, you feel like there is a storm in your stomach that does not feel good at all. At other times, you feel warm and fuzzy.

All these feelings are part of being human. If you understand how you are feeling, you can make better choices about how you react.

Can you draw a picture of how you are feeling right now?

Exercise 2

When you speak to other people like your friends, family, and teachers, you can make them feel good or bad depending on how you treat them.

Sometimes, your friend may be sad and could use your help to feel better. At other times, your friend may be happy, which means it's a great time to have fun together!

Looking at people's faces and bodies can tell you a lot about how they are feeling today.

Can you label which feelings listed here match the faces shown below?

Angry. Happy. Sad. Frustrated. Disgusted. Surprised. Shy. Scared.

Exercise 3

It can be difficult to talk about how you feel.

When you do not have the words to label how you feel, you can describe your emotions so that people around you know how their actions and behavior may affect you.

You can tell people how you feel by letting them know what is happening in your body when you feel a type of emotion. Write down how your body feels inside or what your body does when you are:

- Angry
- Happy
- Sad
- Frustrated
- Disgusted
- Surprised
- Shy
- Scared

Happy.

Sad.

Angry.

Frustrated. *(Feeling frustrated means that you are annoyed because you cannot change something that is not going the way you want it to.)*

Surprised.

Disgusted. *(Being disgusted is the feeling people get when something is gross.)*

Shy.

Scared.

Exercise 4

Let's play a game of pretend. The following stories describe different situations. Draw a picture of how each story made you feel.

Your friend found a frog in your backyard. They ask you if you want to touch the frog and hold it close to you.

Your friend found a frog.
https://pixabay.com/vectors/frog-toad-water-green-frog-6026117/

You fell off a bicycle, and your friends laughed at you.

Falling off your bicycle might cause negative feelings.
https://pixabay.com/vectors/bicycle-small-vehicle-bike-cycle-1456759/

Your parents bought you your favorite toy for your birthday.

Birthdays are a cause for celebration.
https://pixabay.com/vectors/cake-candles-birthday-purple-icing-308576/

You are on a rollercoaster that is going very fast.

Rollercoasters can be very fast.
https://pixabay.com/vectors/rollercoaster-roller-coaster-156027/

Your brother, sister, or friend ate some of your Halloween candy when you were not looking.

Trick-or-treating can help you collect a lot of candy.
https://pixabay.com/vectors/pumpkin-halloween-jack-o-lantern-2504236/

You are late on your first day of school.

Schools can help you learn.
https://pixabay.com/vectors/school-building-education-property-295210/

Exercise 5

What is your favorite color?

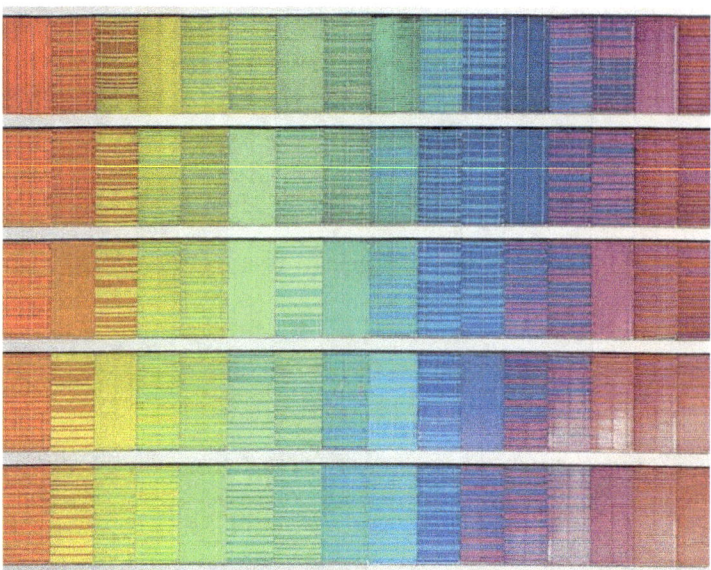

People can have the same favorite color

https://unsplash.com/photos/pRZVCSTqje4?utm_source=unsplash&utm_medium=referral&utm_content=creditShareLink

That's a great color! Some people like your favorite color, too. Other people do not like it as much as you do, and that's fine.

Can you write down how these colors make you feel?

Exercise 6

Sometimes, your feelings can feel quite big, like a giant elephant.

Your feelings can feel as big as an elephant.

https://pixabay.com/vectors/elephant-animal-jungle-savannah-1598359/

Sometimes your feelings can be very teeny-tiny, like a little bitty mouse.

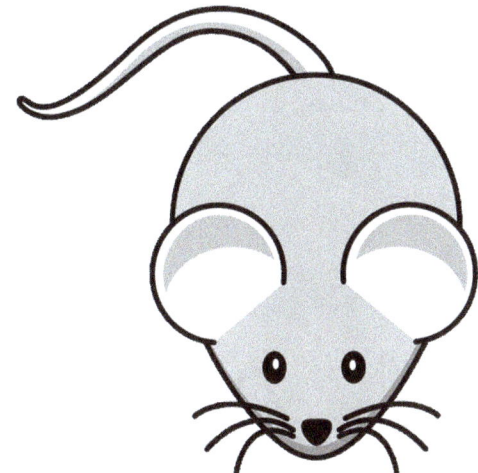

Your feelings can also feel as tiny as a mouse.

https://pixabay.com/vectors/mouse-grey-mammal-rodent-whiskers-303878/

Some things make you happy, and other things can make you sad. Some things can make you very sad, and other things can make you a little bit sad.

How big or small your feelings are is known as intensity. Big feelings are very intense. Small feelings are not so intense. Color in how intense your feelings are for each of the following stories.

Green = Not intense.

Orange = A little intense.

Yellow = Medium intense.

Red = Very intense.

Your friend or sibling hid the TV remote from you. Write down how you felt. Color in how intense that feeling is using green, yellow, orange, or red.

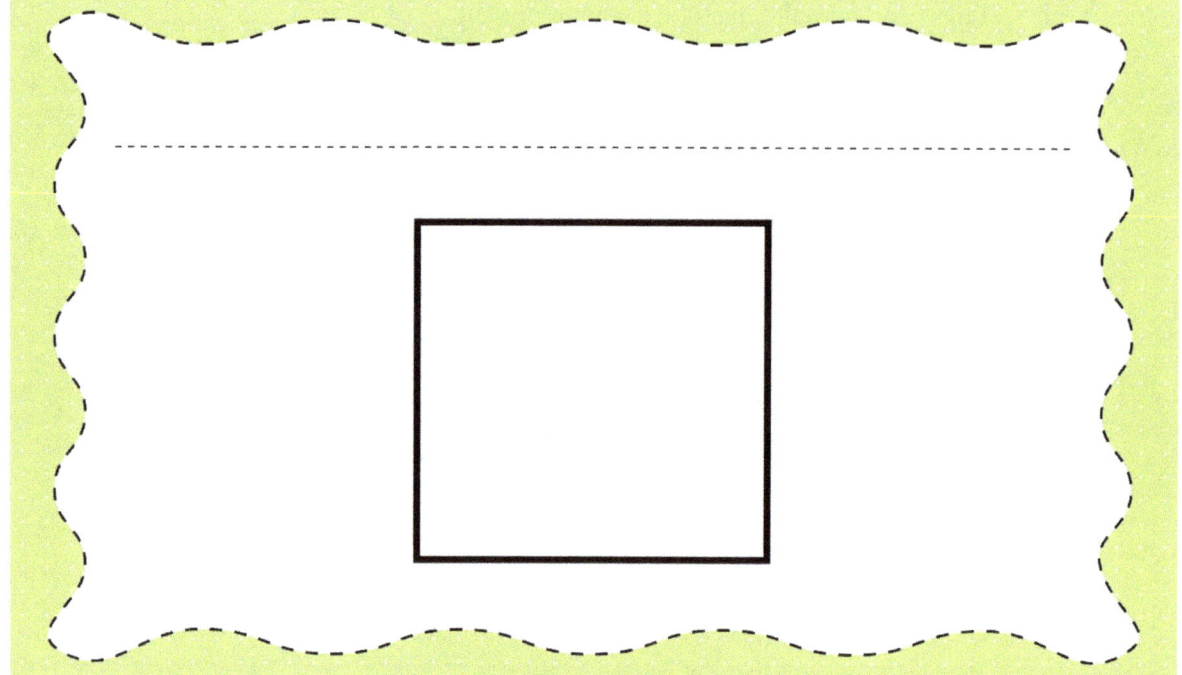

The ice cream cone that you just bought falls on the ground. Write down how you feel. Color in how intense that feeling is using green, yellow, orange, or red.

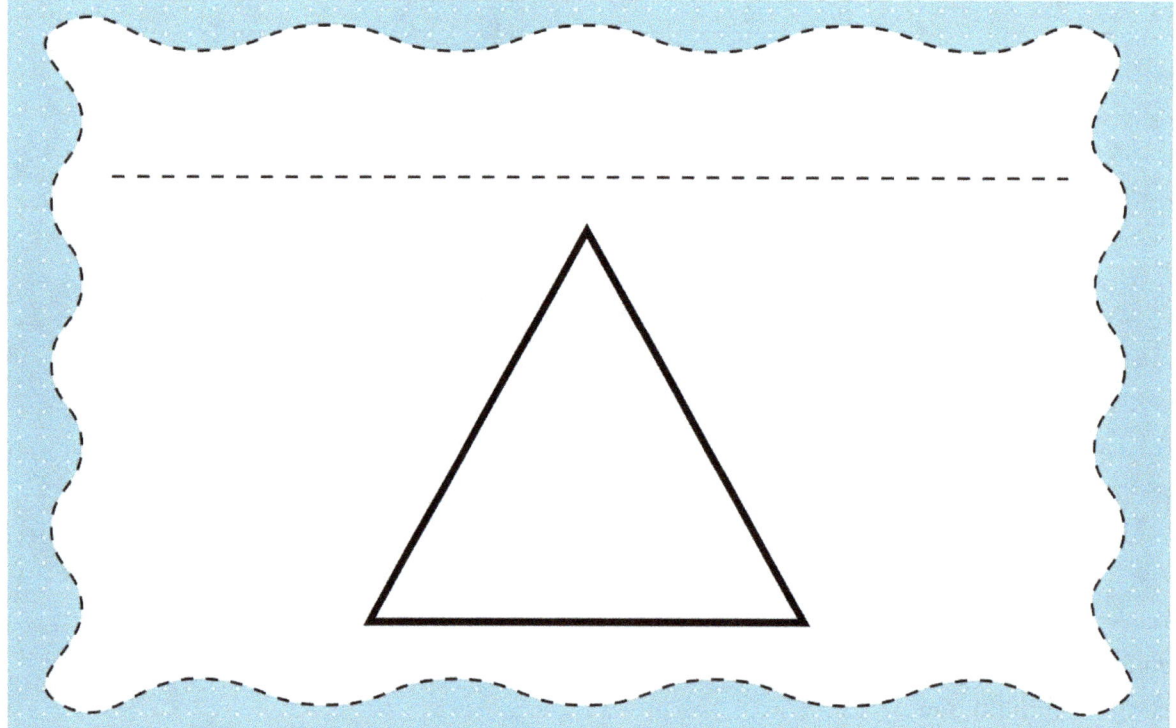

Your teacher or your parents yell at you for misbehaving. Write down how you feel. Color in how intense that feeling is using green, yellow, orange, or red.

You are playing a video game with your friend, and you lose. Write down how you feel. Color in how intense that feeling is using green, yellow, orange, or red.

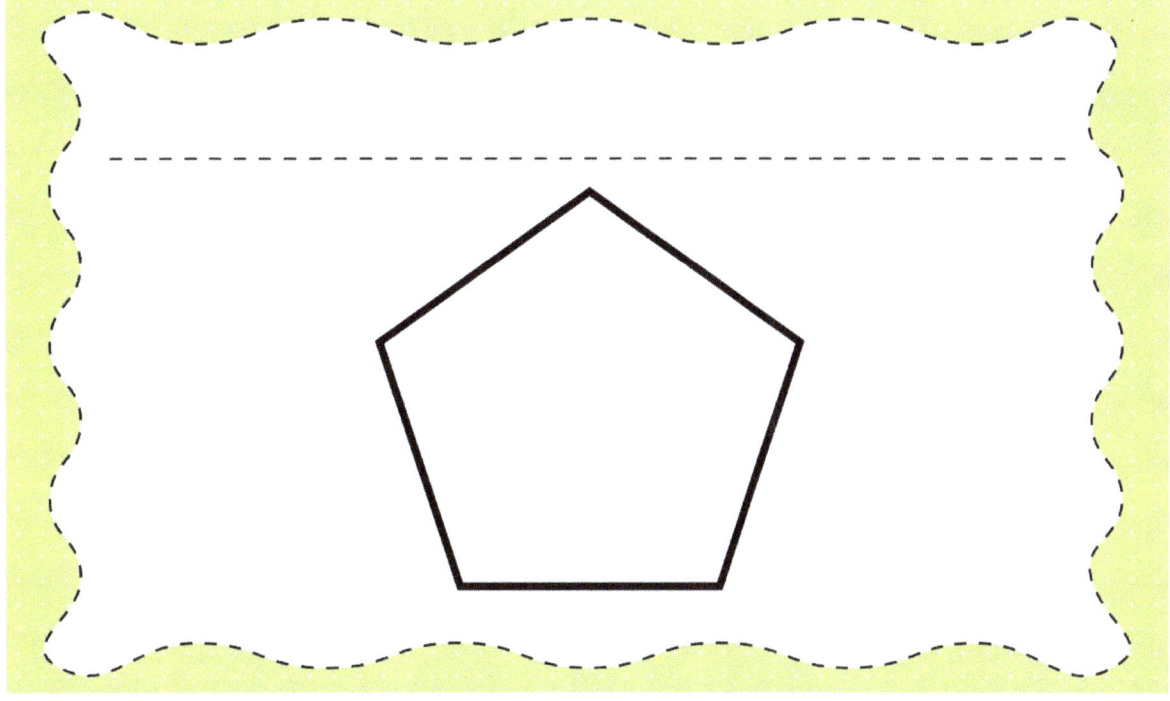

You are playing your favorite sport, and you score the winning point. Write down how you feel. Color in how intense that feeling is using green, yellow, orange, or red.

Exercise 7

Draw a picture of the happiest moment in your life.

Exercise 8

Draw a picture of the saddest moment in your life.

Exercise 9

Who is your favorite superhero? Can you draw a picture of them?

Write down what you like about them. How can you become more like your favorite superhero?

Exercise 10

When was the last time you were happy? Draw a picture of that moment.

When was the last time you were very upset? Draw a picture of that moment.

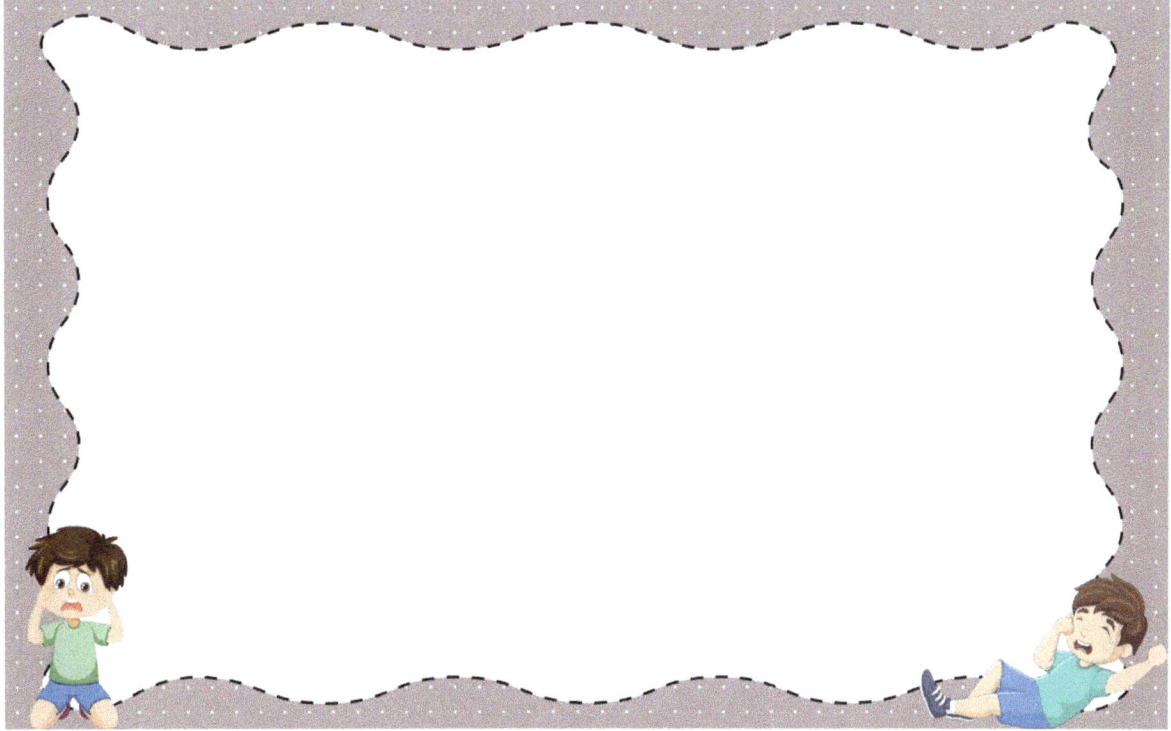

Section 2: Expressing Myself

Five Reasons It Is Important to Express Yourself

Expressing yourself means making your feelings known to the people around you.

Here are five reasons why it is good to express yourself.

- People know what you want, so they can help you if you express yourself.
- Expressing yourself helps you make friends.
- When you do not express yourself, it will make you feel worse inside.
- People will want to talk to you more because they will feel comfortable around you.
- You can learn new things when you express yourself because people will be open to teaching you.

The exercises below will help you learn how to express yourself a lot better.

Exercise 11

Art is one of the best ways to express yourself. By being creative, you can give people a look inside the inner workings of your mind.

Color in the mandala below, by using colors that match your feelings.

Exercise 12

You can express yourself by using your body. Stand up and show your friends a dance of how you are feeling right now.

Exercise 13

For the next activity, you will need some scissors, glue, paper decorations, old magazines, and an old hat. Ask your parents for help.

Cut out pictures from magazines of things that you like or that make you happy. You can even draw the picture you want to use.

Paste these pictures onto your hat to decorate it.

Now you've got a cool hat to show your friends and family what you love!

You can make a vision board, too, if you'd like! For this, you will use cardboard instead of a hat.

Find pictures of what you want to achieve by next year. Maybe you want to join the soccer team, or you want to play an instrument.

Paste the pictures on the cardboard and decorate however you want to.

Put your vision board somewhere you can see it every day to remember what you want to do and achieve.

Exercise 14

Below is a chart labeled with the five main human emotions, which are anger, fear, sadness, disgust, and enjoyment.

Close your eyes and spin your finger over the page. When you are ready, point down the chart. Whichever emotion your finger lands on, make a sound that feels like that emotion.

Remember, do not use words, *only sounds*!

Exercise 15

Some people express themselves using music.

Can you find some old things around the house to make a musical instrument like a drum or a shaker?

Musical notes are what make up a song.

https://pixabay.com/vectors/silhouette-musical-clef-bass-3275055/

Once you have your instrument, make up a song about what you are thinking or feeling right now.

You can sing the song for your family and friends if you want to.

Remember to ask your parents for permission and help before you begin.

Exercise 16

Do you know how to play pretend?

Draw a picture of what you want to be when you grow up.

Now, act out what it would be like to be the person you drew.

Exercise 17

People act in different ways when they feel different emotions or when they are thinking different thoughts. Think about how you act when you're going through different feelings.

Ask a family member or friend to help you with this activity. Below are the columns. One column says, "Looks like," the second column says, "Feels like," and the third column says, "Sounds like."

Looks like	Feels like	Sounds like
SIGHT	TOUCH	HEARING

Write the words "Anger," "Fear," "Sadness," "Disgust," or "Enjoyment" on five pieces of paper. Put these pieces of paper into a bucket or a hat. Shake them up and draw one of the pieces out of the hat.

Your partner will then say, "Looks like," "Feels like," or "Sounds like." Depending on which option your partner chose, you will act out what that feeling looks like, feels like, or sounds like.

You and your partner can take turns choosing an emotion out of the hat and trying to guess the emotion.

Exercise 18

Can you think about something you can do today that will make your parents happy? Draw a picture of your parent's faces if you do this nice thing for them.

Think about what they may say to you if you do this nice thing.

Think about what you will say back to them.

Exercise 19

Can you think about something you can do today that will make your parents upset or disappointed? Draw a picture of your parent's faces if you do the thing that will make them upset.

Think about what you will say.

Think about what they may say.

Exercise 20

What is your favorite movie or TV show?

Draw a picture of your favorite character in the show.

Write down what you would say to them if you ever met them. Think about how you would feel meeting them and what you want them to know about you.

Section 3: Taming My Fears

It's okay to be scared. Fear is a natural emotion that is meant to help you protect yourself. When you are scared, your heart beats faster, and your senses, like sight and hearing, are a lot sharper. Fear is an emotion that evolved from the time when people were living in the wilderness and had to avoid predators. There are still many dangers in the modern world, so your fear is still helpful.

However, fears can turn into phobias. A phobia is when a fear no longer helps you but prevents you from doing something that could benefit you. For example, a fear of heights might stop you from going on a plane to travel the world. Therefore, you must find ways to face your fears so that they do not become a force that holds you back.

Exercise 21

To be able to face your fears, you must first discover what your fears are. What makes you scared more than anything in the world? Is it a big thunderstorm, or is it a creepy-crawly spider?

Draw a fear monster that is made up of all the things you fear the most.

Exercise 22

Many people are afraid of a lot of different things. It is okay to be scared sometimes. Write down ten things that make you feel afraid. Next to each fear, write down how scared you are on a level from 1 to 10. Writing down *10* means that you are extremely afraid, *5* means that you are at a medium level of scared, and *1* means that you are only a little bit afraid.

Fear Crusher

My Goal:

FEAR RATING SCALE

- 10
- 9
- 8
- 7
- 6
- 5
- 4
- 3
- 2
- 1

Exercise 23

If you want to grow into a strong person, you have to find ways to calm yourself down when you are scared. Your imagination can help you face your fears. Imagination is like a superpower that can scare you, but it can also help you not to be afraid. Just like you drew a fear monster, draw a champion who can defeat the fear monster. Think about all the things that make you feel safe and draw them with your champion.

Exercise 24

A lot of things in the world can be scary. Sometimes, things that you think are scary cannot harm you. Someone may be afraid of an earthworm, but most earthworms cannot hurt people. Draw a picture of something you are afraid of but cannot hurt you.

Ask your parents to help you with this exercise. Now, close your eyes and imagine you are sitting in a room with that fear. Think about how your body feels when you are imagining your fear so close to you.

Exercise 25

Even adults have some fears. Ask your parents or your teachers what fears they have and ask them how they face their fears. Maybe, if you are not scared of what they are scared of, you can offer to help them with their fear.

Exercise 26

Everyone needs help sometimes with the things that they fear. Ask your parents to help you with this exercise. Close your eyes and imagine something that you are scared of. How do you feel on the inside when you think about this fear? After you have imagined your fear, open your eyes and hug your parents. Do you feel better? People can help each other when someone feels scared. It is okay to speak to your parents and teachers about your fears.

Hugs can calm your fears.
https://unsplash.com/photos/MRWHSKimBJk?utm_source=unsplash&utm_medium=referral&utm_content=creditShareLink

Exercise 27

Have you ever felt so scared that it feels like your body cannot do anything? There are ways to turn down the fear inside of your body. Close your eyes and imagine something that makes you scared. Think about how your fear makes you feel. After you have imagined your fear, take a deep breath in and count to three. Then, breathe out. Take another deep breath in and then count to three, then breathe out. Repeat this ten times.

How do you feel now after doing some deep breathing? This exercise should help you control your feelings.

Exercise 28

Draw a picture of what it is like to be scared. Next to it, draw a picture of what it is like to feel safe.

How does your body feel on the inside when you are safe, and how does your body feel on the inside when you are scared?

Exercise 29

Think about the last time that you got scared. Draw a picture of the situation or object that made you afraid.

Exercise 30

Now that you have drawn a picture of what made you scared, can you draw a picture of how you got out of that scary situation?

Can you see that your fear did not last forever but only for a tiny moment? It can help to remember that when you are scared, it will not last forever. It is a feeling that will pass.

Section 4: Putting My Anger to Sleep

Everybody gets angry sometimes. Your anger shows you that you are not pleased with a situation, person, or even yourself. People sometimes do things they're not proud of when they are angry, like yelling or fighting.

Even when you are angry, it is not good to hurt people. That's why you need to find healthy ways to deal with your anger.

Exercise 31

Think about the last time you got angry. Draw a picture of what made you angry and what you did when you were angry.

Things that make people angry are called *triggers*. Can you think of some triggers that make you angry?

Exercise 32

This is called the *anger thermometer*. It helps you measure how angry you are.

At the bottom, it is cold, which means that you are not very angry. At the top, it is boiling hot, which means you are so angry it feels like you could explode.

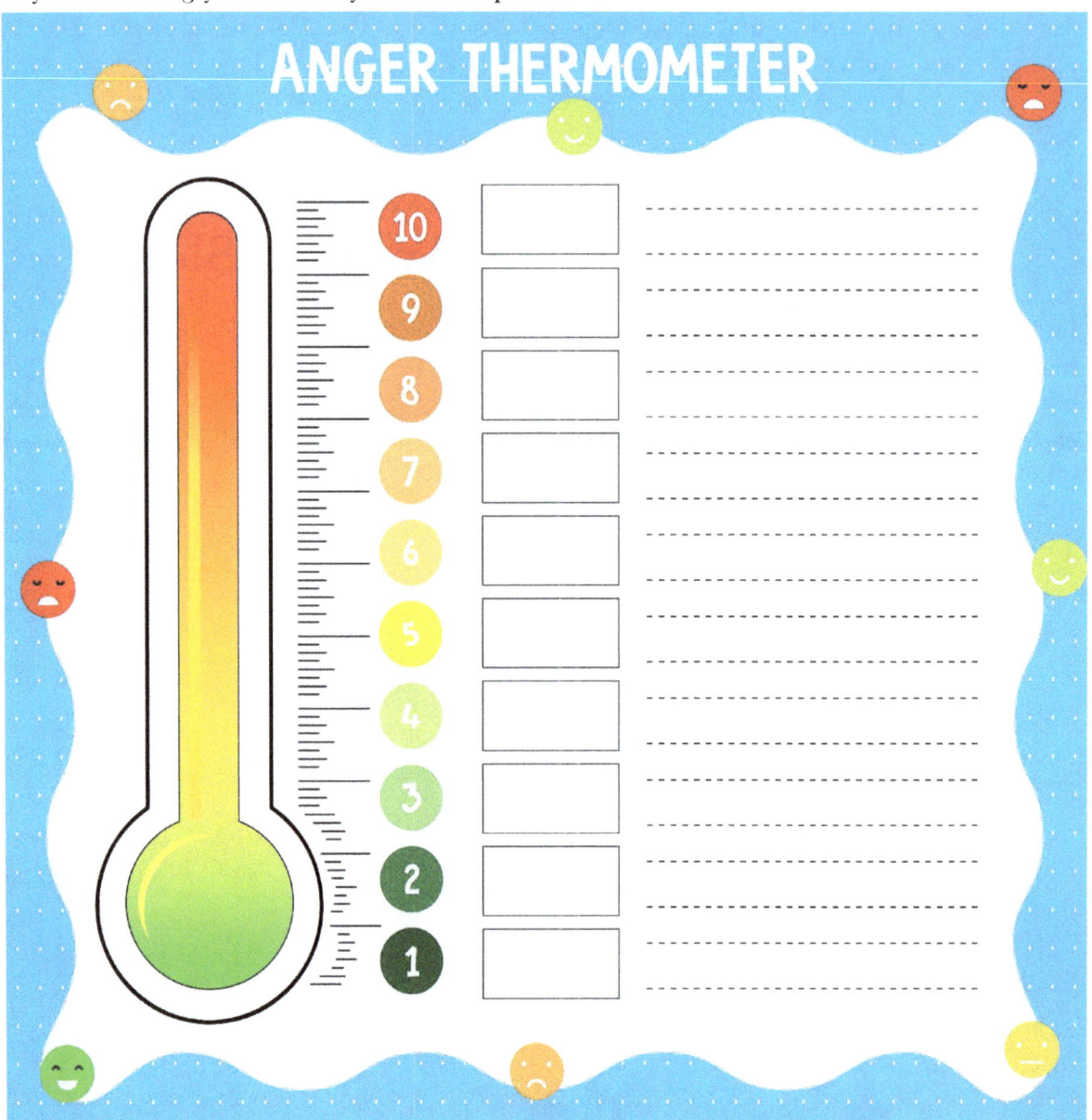

There are ten spaces next to the thermometer. Write down in each space something that makes you angry. At the bottom, write something that makes you a little angry, like maybe losing in a video game.

Then, at the top, write something that makes you extremely angry. At each level of the thermometer, you will write something that makes you angrier and angrier until you reach the highest level of anger at the top.

Exercise 33

Just because you are angry does not mean you can be rude to people or hurt them. You need to find ways to use your words when you are angry. Here are ways you can use your words to talk about your feelings.

Start your sentence with:

"I feel"

After I feel, you can describe your emotions; for example, *I feel angry.*

Once you describe your emotions, you can add "because" followed by the reason you are angry. For example, *"I feel angry because you ate my last piece of chocolate."*

Then you can ask what you would like them to do next time so that you don't get angry. For example, *"Next time, ask me before you eat my chocolate."*

Think about a time you got angry and started crying or screaming. Instead of doing that, write a sentence you could have said to communicate your feelings better.

I feel [ ] because [ ]. Next time I would like it if you [ ].

Exercise 34

Think about the last time you lost your temper. Draw a picture of how it felt right before you got angry. Maybe your chest felt hot, or you were clenching your teeth.

These are signs that you are about to lose your temper. When you feel like this, there are things you can do to calm down so that you use your words to express your anger clearly.

When you feel like this, stand up, stretch, take three deep breaths, and count to ten slowly.

Exercise 35

Physical activities can help you calm down when you are angry or frustrated. Sometimes, you need to take a break and walk away from what is making you angry.

Think about something that makes you angry. Now, go outside and run around your yard for ten laps. Come back and write down how you felt after running.

Exercise 36

Draw a picture of something that makes you happy.

Whenever you get angry, you can use your imagination to remind yourself of what makes you happy. Close your eyes and imagine this picture when you get angry. This picture is your happy place, and you can go there in your mind whenever you want to.

Exercise 37

You can use words to calm down when you are angry. The following sentences are called affirmations or mantras. These are sentences you can repeat when you feel angry or frustrated. Say these sentences out loud.

- I am calm.
- I can handle this.
- I am going to be okay.
- I am relaxed.
- I am patient.
- I can get through any situation.

Say these affirmations when you feel yourself getting angry.

Exercise 38

Draw the face of someone who is angry. Think about their eyes, mouth, and any other parts of their face.

Write down what you can do if your face looks like this.

Exercise 39

Not everyone gets angry about the same things. That's why it is important to tell people what makes you angry.

Can you think of some things that make you angry?

Now, think of some things that make your best friend angry.

Think about what makes your parents and teacher angry.

What are the differences between what makes you angry and what makes your parents angry?

Exercise 40

Color the box below with colors and patterns you think look like anger.

Now, color in this box with colors and patterns you think look like happiness.

Section 5: Keeping My Worries Away

Do you ever worry about things that are happening in your life? Maybe you have a test coming up or a big sports game you are playing. Sometimes, something terrible can happen, like your friend breaking their arm, so you worry about them.

Worrying about people and events that happen in your life is normal because it shows that you care. Worrying does not feel good and can cause you to take actions that do not help you. The following exercises will give you the tools to worry less and face challenges head-on.

Worrying does not feel good, but you can do things to help you stop worrying.
https://pxhere.com/en/photo/778587

Exercise 41

If you worry for too long, it can cause *anxiety*.

Anxiety is when you are very nervous about the future or when you worry about things that you cannot control.

Anxiety happens when you think about the future and problems too much. Your brain can paint pictures that are sometimes not real.

For this activity, you will need some glitter, a jar, and water. Pour some water and glitter into a jar. Whenever you feel like your thoughts are running away with you, shake the jar and watch the glitter slowly fall. This can help you to calm down.

Exercise 42

What causes you to worry? Draw a "worry monster" made up of all the things that make you worry.

Exercise 43

Now that you have drawn a "worry monster," draw a "worry hero" with all the things you love to do that make you calm down and feel relaxed.

Think about which of the things you do that calm you down can help you when you are feeling worried.

Exercise 44

When you worry, often it can be because you are thinking negatively about things. Changing the way you think about problems to be more positive can help you worry less.

For example, instead of thinking, "What if I fail my test tomorrow?" you can think, "I am prepared for my test because I studied hard."

Always think positive and believe in yourself when you're studying.
https://www.pexels.com/photo/diverse-kids-studying-together-at-home-5905846/

Here are some sentences; can you write some ways to think of them positively instead?
- "Maybe my friends don't like me."
- "My mother is going to be angry because I broke a glass by mistake."
- "I am going to be late for school tomorrow."
- "I won't be able to finish my project in time for school."

Exercise 45

Do you ever feel afraid to be in your room alone? Does it feel like someone is in there watching you? Many children, and sometimes even adults, have the same worry.

Being alone in your room can be scary.
https://unsplash.com/photos/b_GtasP517U?utm_source=unsplash&utm_medium=referral&utm_content=creditShareLink

Your worries can always be decreased if you take action. Before you go to sleep, ask your parents to check your room with you. Look inside the cupboards. Look under the bed and look in all the corners of the room.

Now you will see that there is no one there, so there is no need to worry.

Exercise 46

Reading a book can stop you from worrying too much. Ask your parents to take you to the library or the bookstore to get a book you like. When you are feeling worried, take out your book to read about wonderful adventures!

Exercise 47

Journaling

Do you know what a journal is?

A journal is a book where you can write down your worries, emotions, thoughts, plans, and achievements. Some people draw or paste pictures into their journals as well.

Journaling can help you think deeper about the way you are feeling and what is making you feel that way.

Keeping a journal can also help you keep track of all the changes in your life.

Sometimes, it can be difficult to talk to people. A journal can help you get out all the thoughts that are hard to speak about out loud.

Writing in a journal every day can help you control your emotions and your behavior better.

Creating Your Journal

Ask your parents to get you a copybook journal. You can decorate this copybook with pictures, stickers, or whatever else you like.

Writing about Your Thoughts and Feelings

Every evening, or when you are feeling worried, write how you are feeling in your journal.

If you don't like writing, you can draw pictures of how you feel. This will help you to understand your worries a bit better so that you can find solutions.

Exercise 48

What makes you worry more than anything else? Write down why this makes you worry so much.

Exercise 49

Your imagination can be good for you, but it can also be bad for you. Remember that your thoughts are not always real.

Your imagination can make you more creative.
https://pixabay.com/vectors/child-drawing-childhood-imagination-5729019/

Think about something that makes you worry. Now, imagine a giant bubble surrounding that worry and carrying it far away into the sky. Take a deep breath in. How do you feel? You can use your mind to fight your worries.

Exercise 50

What do you love to do, or what is your favorite hobby? Write down a list of your hobbies, like drawing, reading, or playing outside.

Sometimes, when you are worrying, you need a break. Hobbies can distract you from your worries.

Exercise 51

How much can you count? What's the biggest number you have ever counted up to? When your thoughts feel like they are filling up your brain, start counting. Count slowly and out loud until you begin feeling better.

Section 6: Anxiety Fighters

Anxiety is when your worries build up so much that they fill your mind. This makes your body feel uncomfortable.

Anxiety can be caused by thoughts about the future or by thinking about things that you cannot control. Don't worry because there are many ways to help you deal with anxiety.

Exercise 52

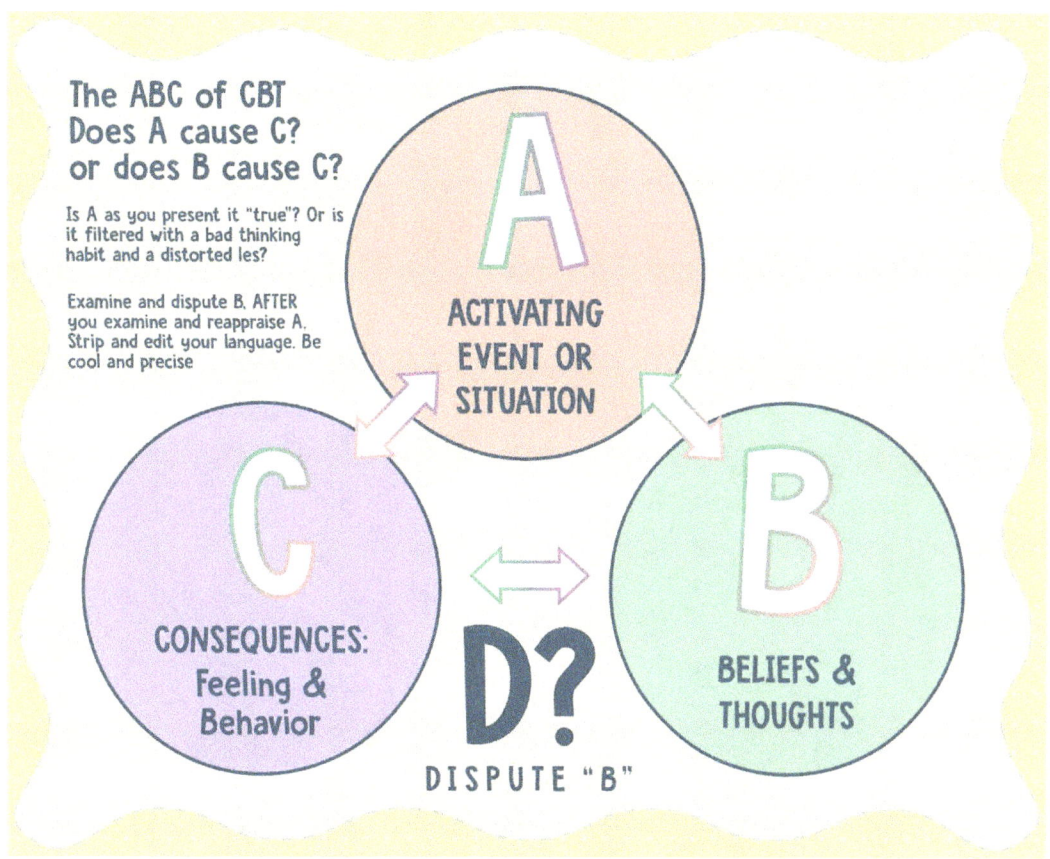

Anxiety is when you feel nervous or uncomfortable because there are too many thoughts going through your mind.

What do you do when you feel nervous?

What do you think can help you stop feeling nervous?

The ABC method is a tool that helps with anxiety. The ABC method takes your negative thoughts and turns them into positive thoughts. "A" stands for "Activating event." That means what thing happened to cause the event? "B" stands for "Beliefs about an event." "C" stands for "Consequences." Consequences are what happens after you take a certain action. For example, the consequence of eating too much sugar is cavities in your teeth.

Here's how to use the ABC method.

Start with "A" or the Activating event. Write down an event you can remember that caused anxiety.

Now "B" for "Beliefs about an event." Write down what you were thinking when the event was happening.

Finally, "C." Write down how these thoughts made you act and how they made you feel.

This exercise will help you understand why you are having certain thoughts and feelings so you can come up with better solutions.

Exercise 53

Now that you've applied the ABC method, can you write down some positive thoughts that you could have had in the same situation?

Draw a picture of your negative and positive thoughts of the same situation next to one another. Compare the two to see what changes you could have made in your mind.

Exercise 54

Let's play pretend. Imagine that you are an anxiety detective. Detectives ask people questions so they can solve problems.

Detectives use clues to solve problems.
https://pixabay.com/vectors/detective-searching-man-search-1424831/

Pretend to be a detective to ask yourself some questions. Ask yourself what makes you feel anxious and why it makes you feel anxious. This will help you find the cause of your anxiety.

Exercise 55

Talking to someone you trust about your anxieties is helpful. It is not good to keep everything bottled up. Write down a list of things that make you anxious and share that list with a parent or an adult you trust, like a teacher.

Exercise 56

Create a worry jar for your anxieties. This can help you keep track of all the thoughts and actions that cause anxiety. Certain thoughts and events that cause anxiety are known as *triggers*. By knowing your triggers, you give yourself more power to fight anxiety.

Adding your worries to a jar can help you find solutions for them.
https://unsplash.com/photos/b29z0iltxk4

    Find an old jar. Whenever you are feeling anxious or having an uncomfortable thought, write it on a piece of paper and put it in the jar. At the end of the week, you can go through all the pieces of paper in the jar to find solutions and plans to help you cope with your anxiety with the help of your parents. It can be hard to think clearly when you are anxious, so this helps you think about your worries when your mind is calmer and clearer.

Exercise 57

Talking to your friends can also help you fight anxiety. Ask your parents to organize a short meeting every week to talk to a group of friends. You and your friends can share your worries and work together to tackle your anxieties over different issues. Your friends might be able to give you good advice and may even have gone through similar situations themselves.

Talking to your friends can help you find solutions to your worries.
https://www.pexels.com/photo/children-in-circle-formation-11429489/

Exercise 58

Can you think of your favorite smells? Maybe you like the smell of flowers or the smell of a certain type of soap. Using different scents and smells to calm you down is called *aromatherapy*.

Flowers can be used as a form of aromatherapy.
https://www.pexels.com/photo/close-up-shot-of-colorful-tulips-in-white-basket-7156469/

Get a spray bottle. Take some citrus peels and pleasant-smelling flowers and put them inside the bottle. You can even get some nice-smelling oils and add them to the mixture. After you have put the flower petals and orange peels into the spray bottle, fill it with water. Give the bottle a good, strong shake. When you spray it, a pleasant smell will come out. This smell will calm you down.

Exercise 59

Spending time outside eases anxiety. When you are indoors too often, it can feel like the walls are closing in and that your thoughts are becoming too noisy. Ask your parents to take you to a park or a nature reserve.

Walking for a little bit in a natural environment and getting some fresh air can clear your mind of negative thoughts.

Exercise 60

Touch is a great tool to help you to fight your anxiety. Next time you are feeling overwhelmed by your thoughts, take off your shoes, go outside, and stand barefoot on the sand or grass. Focus on how the ground feels in between your toes, and take a few deep breaths until you calm down.

Feeling the grass can help you calm down.
https://www.pexels.com/photo/a-person-s-feet-on-green-grass-13724474/

Exercise 61

Keeping fit and exercising also combats anxiety. Write down a list of your favorite sports. Choose one or two sports on the list that you like a lot. Ask your parents to help you find a team in your neighborhood that you can join. Maybe you could join a team at your school.

After doing all these exercises, have you learned anything new about your anxiety?

Doing sports can help you feel better.
https://www.pexels.com/photo/football-players-playing-at-field-15203/

Section 7: My Zen Zone

A *Zen zone* is a mind state where you can find calmness and peace free from anxiety, sadness, and anger. Entering a Zen zone can be done with mindfulness activities. Mindfulness exercises help you slow down your thoughts so that you can better understand yourself without too many distractions.

For most of the day, your mind works on autopilot because you are going along and reacting to what is happening around you. Mindfulness is like taking the steering wheel of your brain so that your mind is no longer driving you, but you are driving your mind.

Exercise 62

Coloring can help a lot when it comes to reducing anxiety. What types of pictures do you like to color? Below are some pictures of mandalas. Previously, you colored in a mandala with emotions on it. Now, you can color in these mandalas however you like. Use a lot of different colors and have fun!

Exercise 63

People feel their emotions in their bodies. Think about how you feel when you are angry. Maybe it feels like you are getting hot, or your heart is beating fast while your jaw is clenched. Now think about when you are happy. You may feel light and a bit tingly inside.

Doing a body scan can help you feel your emotions better. Lay down in a comfortable spot. Take a few deep breaths in and out.

With your eyes closed, bring your attention to your toes. How do they feel?

Move up to your ankles, then your knees, and then your hips. Continue up until your belly button and then to your chest and arms. Finally, bring your attention to your head. How do all the parts of your body feel? Where does it feel tight, and where is it relaxed?

Exercise 64

When you feel like your thoughts are piling up, slow your mind down with some breathing. Sit with your legs crossed and your back straight. Set a timer for five minutes. You can ask your parents to join in. Breathe in deep through your mouth and out through your nose. A lot of thoughts will pop up in your mind when you feel yourself losing focus, so bring your attention back to your breath. After five minutes of doing this, how do you feel?

Meditating with your parents can quiet your thoughts.
https://www.pexels.com/photo/mother-and-son-doing-yoga-together-6951647/

Exercise 65

Go and sit outside and close your eyes. First, start with what you are touching. What kind of chair are you sitting on? If you are on the ground, think about how the ground feels. How does your skin feel? Is it sweaty, dry, warm, or cold?

What sounds do you hear? Are there birds around? Do you hear people talking, or maybe some cars?

Think about what you can smell. Do you smell flowers or food?

Lick your lips. What can you taste? Is it sweet, sour, or bitter?

Exercise 66

A mindfulness practice that you can do easily is a room scan. Walk into your bedroom and stand in the doorway. Look around and make a list in your mind of whatever you can see.

Now leave your room and go into the kitchen. Make a list in your mind of whatever you saw in your room. Go back to your room and make a list again of what you saw. Do you see new items? What differences are there between the first time you went into your room and the second time? You can do this activity when you are feeling stressed.

Exercise 67

Do you like drawing or painting? Get a piece of paper and some paint or coloring pencils. Go sit outside and draw what you see. Maybe there is a tree or an ant hill. Take your time and draw or paint all the details. How do you feel after making your painting or drawing?

Exercise 68

Go outside for fifteen minutes and write down everything you hear. Make sure that you get permission from a grownup, or you can ask an adult to go outside with you. Do this exercise every day for about a week. Compare your lists. What differences are there? Are there any changes in what you heard? Did you hear more at the start of the week or at the end of the week?

Exercise 69

Lie down outside on a sunny day when there are some clouds in the sky. Or, at night, you can lie down on the ground and observe the stars. Ask your parents to join you. Make some shapes with the clouds, or guess what shapes the clouds look like to help you relax.

Finding shapes in the sky can help you relax.
https://www.pexels.com/photo/scenic-view-of-clouds-during-dawn-1269777/

Exercise 70

Walking is a great activity to clear your mind. Set up an obstacle course in your garden. Get cardboard and set it all around your yard. Jump from one piece of cardboard to the next. Try not to touch the ground. This is a fun game you can play with friends.

Exercise 71

Do you like music? What is your favorite song? Ask your parents to play your favorite song and make up a dance you can do together. Whenever you are feeling down, play the song and do the dance. If you want, you can make up many dances for many songs.

Dancing with your family can make you feel better.
https://www.pexels.com/photo/happy-family-dancing-4609052/

Section 8: Healthy Habits, Happy Minds

Keeping your mind and body healthy requires you to work on yourself every day.

Activities or behaviors that you repeat every day are called habits.

When you do something every day for long enough, you do not have to think about it. For example, you might brush your teeth every night before you go to bed.

Think about if you wanted to become good at playing a musical instrument. You cannot play an instrument for one day and think that you will become a great musician. You have to practice every day because you will get better slowly over time.

Good habits are activities or actions you take every day that help make you a better person. Good habits will make you healthier, smarter, and stronger, and they will let you help the people around you.

Practicing good habits every day will take you closer to being anything you want to be in life.

If you want to be happy, make friends, and do well in school, you need to think about your daily habits. These habits will include eating healthy, getting enough sleep, and having social interactions. Self-care is very important because if you feel good about yourself, you take greater actions in the world.

Exercise 72

Health is not just about your body. Health is about your emotions, your social groups, and your mind as well. Below is a wellness wheel. Each section of the wheel deals with a different part of yourself. The wheel is divided to show your emotional needs, intellectual needs, social needs, physical needs, and spiritual needs.

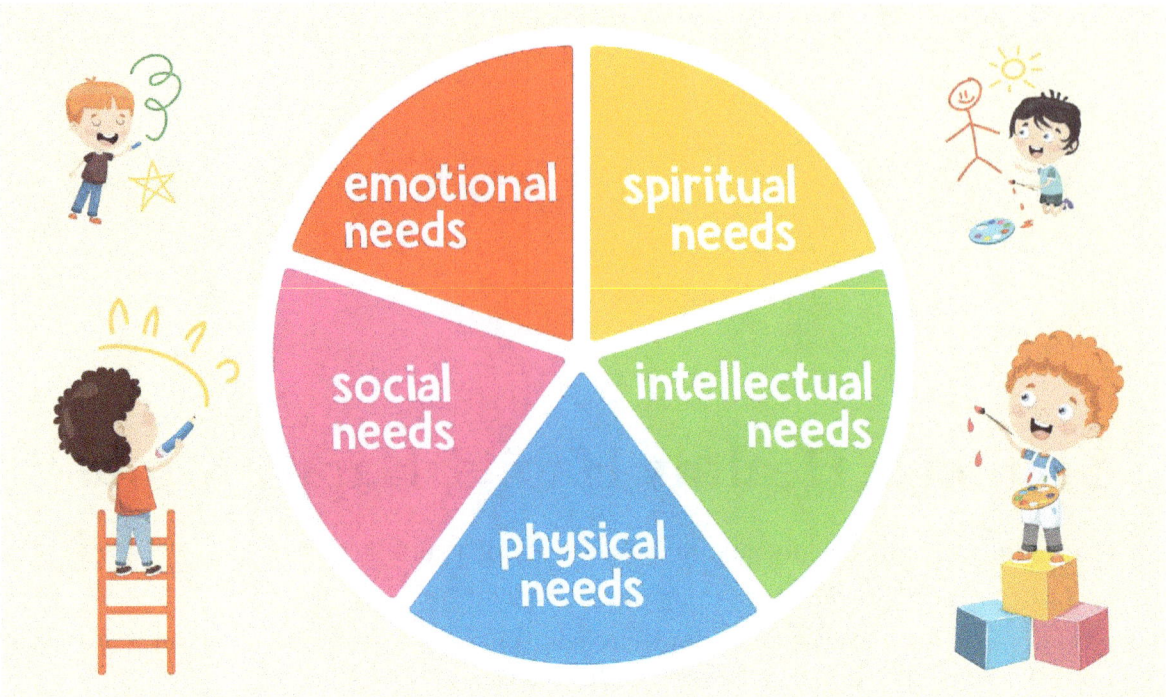

- Your emotional needs are everything needed to make you feel happy.
- Your physical needs are everything that makes your body healthy.
- Your social needs are everything you need from your family and friends to love them better.
- Your spiritual needs are everything that you believe in, like your religion.
- Your intellectual needs are everything that makes you smarter.

Write down what you need for each section of the wellness wheel.

Exercise 73

Planning your time can help you build healthy habits. Ask your parents to help you draw up a schedule to follow daily. This schedule should include time to do your homework, time for bed, time to wash and brush your teeth, as well as time to have fun and do chores. If you follow a schedule, you can get everything done that you need to in the day.

Exercise 74

Below is a wellness tracker.

This tracker should be filled in every day. In the first column, fill in the date.

The second column is to fill in what good things you did for yourself. This includes activities like cleaning your room or exercising.

The fourth column is to note something good you did for others, like sharing food with your friends.

The last column is for a bad habit you want to change. Maybe you left your clothes lying around, and it upsets your parents.

This can help you keep track of all of your good and bad habits so you can keep improving.

Exercise 75

Read the following sentences. Can you think of things to say to yourself when you have these negative thoughts?

- I am useless and can't do anything right.
- I am not smart enough.
- I am not good enough.
- I am always doing the wrong thing.
- I can never achieve my goals.

Thinking positively can help you succeed in all areas of your life.

Exercise 76

In the morning, when you are getting ready for school, look in the mirror and say five good things about yourself. This can be something like "I look good today" or "I am strong."

These sentences are called *affirmations*. They help you create a better mindset for yourself.

Write down five affirmations that you can repeat below.

Exercise 77

To become closer to your family or friends, you must talk to them every day. Compliments are words you say to people that make them feel good. For example, you can tell someone that they have really beautiful shoes on.

When you wake up in the morning, write down three names. These names are people that you will give compliments to when you see them. Remember to be nice to people, and people will be more polite to you.

Being kind to others will cause others to be more polite to you.

https://unsplash.com/photos/VSYVwkHT-dg?utm_source=unsplash&utm_medium=referral&utm_content=creditShareLink

Exercise 78

Being thankful is a great way to keep a healthy mind. Write down ten things you are grateful for. Maybe you are thankful that you got a good meal or that you have a warm bed. It can be an event that happened or something someone said. There is a lot to be thankful for.

Exercise 79

Eating healthy is very good for your body and mind. Write down your favorite fruits and vegetables. Every morning you can help your parents pack your lunch and remind them to add some healthy food.

Exercise 80

What do you do before you go to sleep? It is good to have a routine to clean yourself up and relax before bed. Ask your parents to help you set up a nighttime schedule. The schedule should include washing your face, brushing your teeth, putting on pajamas, and reading a book.

Exercise 81

Do you exercise? What is your favorite exercise? With the help of your parents, draw up an exercise routine to do when you have free time in the day. It will look something like this:

- 10 jumping jacks.
- 10 push-ups.
- 10 sit-ups.

Do these exercises every day with your parents.

Section 9: Conquering My Biggest Challenges

In life, you will constantly encounter challenges. No matter how much your parents love you, they will not always be there to help you face your challenges. That's why you must learn how to conquer your challenges with problem-solving skills. The following exercises will give you the tools needed to solve your problems. By solving your problems, you will become more independent.

This independence will help you create better relationships with your friends and family and will help you boost your self-esteem. Self-esteem is the way you think about yourself. When you think about yourself in a positive way, you have high self-esteem. When you think about yourself in a negative way, you have low self-esteem.

Exercise 82

To know what your biggest challenges are, you first need to know what you want from your life. You need to set goals and think about where you see yourself in the future. A tool that can help point you in the right direction is a vision board.

Get a large piece of paper or cardboard. Cut out some pictures of what you want your life to be like. Maybe you want to finish school, or perhaps you want to live in a big house. Stick those pictures onto the paper or cardboard. You can write words and sentences if you want to describe them, as well. Decorate it however you like. Stick your vision board on your bedroom wall in a place where you can see it clearly. Think about what you can do every day to achieve your vision.

Exercise 83

You will face challenges daily. Sometimes the challenge will be big, and sometimes it will be small.

The table below has six columns. The first column says, "Problem of the day." Write down a challenge that you want to conquer for the day. The next three columns are "Step 1", "Step 2", and "Step 3". Break your problem into three steps that you can complete for the day. The next column says, "End result." In this column, write down what happened after you followed your three-step plan. The last column says "Improvements." In the last column, write down how you can solve the problem in a better way the next time it comes up.

Exercise 84

Positive affirmations help you face your challenges better. Below are some affirmations. Underneath each affirmation is a shape. Repeat the affirmation while coloring in the shape. Use any color that makes you happy.

I am a star.

I am whole.

I can do anything.

I can climb any mountain.

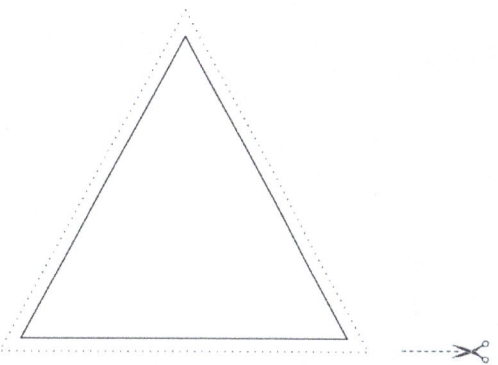

You can draw these shapes and repeat these affirmations whenever you want to.

Exercise 85

It's time to play a game of pretend. You forgot about an assignment and realized that it is due tomorrow. You have a lot of stress, and it is going to be hard work to finish the project. Your parents are there to help you with the project. The project is going to add a lot to your grades, so you must get it done. Can you write down the best ways that you can solve the problem?

Exercise 86

Being out of a soccer game doesn't mean you can't be supportive.
https://www.pexels.com/photo/action-ball-field-game-274506/

You are in a soccer match, and you hurt yourself. The coach takes you out of the game and puts you on the bench. The score is still 0-0, but your team has a good chance of winning. You are upset and angry that you are on the bench. Write down some ways that you can support your team from the sidelines. Also, write down ways in which you can control your emotions to manage your feelings about being taken off the field.

Exercise 87

Your parents have taken away your favorite toy, tablet, or video game as a punishment because you were misbehaving. You are upset and sitting in your room bored. Write down some ways that you can manage your emotions. Also, think about how you can prevent yourself from being bored. Now, write down some ways you can make your parents happy so that they can give you back your toy, tablet, or video game.

Exercise 88

Can you think of any problems you faced in the past? Write down the problem and how you overcame it.

Write down the worst thing that could have happened if the problem continued.

Now, write down the *best thing* that could have happened if you solved the problem better.

Think about future problems. In the future, how can you apply what you learned in this problem?

Exercise 89

Draw a picture of where you see yourself by the end of the year. This has to be the best possible version of yourself if you achieve all your goals, like getting good grades or making new friends.

Think about how you can make sure that that version of yourself exists in the future. What habits can you change? What habits can you start? What decisions can you make daily?

Exercise 90

Ask your parents to help you set up a scavenger hunt. Your parents should hide a toy somewhere in the yard. Around the house, they should write down some clues about where the toy is.

Once the scavenger hunt is set up, you can use your problem-solving skills to figure out the clues and find the hidden item.

You can do this with your friends as well. You and your friends can take turns setting up a scavenger hunt for each other.

Exercise 91

This is a competition where you can play against your friends. Ask your parents to get you some glue and sticks. These sticks can be toothpicks, match sticks, or ice cream sticks. You and your friends can divide into two or three teams. You must work together to build a tall tower out of sticks and glue. Whoever builds the tallest tower wins.

Section 10: Embracing Myself

Nobody is perfect. Everybody has flaws, and everybody makes mistakes. Some people put their clothes on backward, and other people have smelly feet. Some people talk way too loudly, and others whisper super softly. No matter the flaws you have or the mistakes you make, you are still worth so much in the world! Accepting yourself with all your imperfections is how you can build high self-esteem. Your self-esteem and self-image come from the way you think about yourself.

No one is going to love you more than you love yourself. No one will spend more time with you than yourself because you live inside your body. That's why you need to make sure that you love and care for yourself, even in times when you are feeling low.

Exercise 92

Here is a list of 20 different positive traits. Circle the traits that you feel best describe you and your personality.

1. Kind
2. Strong
3. Hard-working
4. Humble
5. Beautiful
6. Fast
7. Athletic
8. Intelligent
9. Caring
10. Loving
11. Friendly
12. Funny
13. Neat
14. Brave

15. Curious
16. Charming
17. Interesting
18. Creative
19. Unselfish
20. Adventurous

Now that you've circled some of these characteristics, you should draw a picture of yourself that represents these traits.

Exercise 93

Now that you have circled some of the positive traits mentioned above, can you think of other positive characteristics about yourself?

It's important to remind yourself of your positive traits.

https://unsplash.com/photos/g3KbcDWrBUM?utm_source=unsplash&utm_medium=referral&utm_content=creditShareLink

Write down some positive things about yourself with some colorful pens and stick them on a mirror. Every time you look in that mirror, remind yourself how amazing you are!

Exercise 94

Sometimes, it can be difficult to think of good things to say about yourself. Ask your friends and family what they like about you. Write down what they said to remember that there are people in your life who love you and think that you are incredible.

Exercise 95

A support system is the people that help you in your life. This can be your friends, family, and your teachers. Below is a tree with some empty spaces for names. This is your support system tree. Write down all the people who care about you in the empty spaces provided.

Exercise 96

Ask your parents if you can decorate your notebook or journal. This book will be your compliment journal. Decorate the book with whatever you want. This can be pictures of stuff that you like or with your favorite colors. Every day, in the morning, write a compliment to yourself. *A compliment is something that you like about yourself.* This can remind you that you are a person who should be treated well and who can achieve anything you set your mind to.

Exercise 97

Reminding yourself of your strengths can help you become more confident.
https://unsplash.com/photos/_XTY6lD8jgM?utm_source=unsplash&utm_medium=referral&utm_content=creditShareLink

Think about what you are good at. This can be a sport or even a subject at school. It may even be a video game that you are good at. Write down why you are so good at this activity and how you can become better at it.

Exercise 98

Think of a victory dance that you can do when you win a game or achieve something great. Show your victory dance to your friends and family. Whenever you succeed at something, do this victory dance to celebrate.

Exercise 99

Can you think of a moment in the past when you did something great or achieved one of your goals? It is amazing that you were able to do that! Draw a picture of the moment when you achieved something great in the past.

Exercise 100

One of the ways you can boost your confidence is by doing a power pose. This is the pose that superheroes do when they arrive to defeat the bad guy! Whenever you are feeling down or weak, do this pose. Stand up tall. Spread your legs wide, then raise your right fist into the sky as high as you can. Do you feel the power?

Exercise 101

Ask your parents for some old magazines and newspapers. Think about all your strengths and the things that make you great. Now, cut out some pictures that represent those strengths and stick them onto a poster. Look at that poster whenever you feel down or are doubting yourself.

Bonus Section: Thought Challenge

This bonus section is the final exercise in the book.

Congratulations! You have worked through all the exercises and are on your way to making your life so much better. The final exercise is a checklist for you to work through daily. This checklist will show you how well you are doing and whether you are sticking to the lessons you've worked through in the book. This checklist should be done at the end of every day as a way to track your progress and your daily activities.

Checklist

- ☐ Did I think about how I feel today?
- ☐ Did I do something nice for myself today?
- ☐ Did I feel anxious at any time during the day?
- ☐ Did I implement any of the tools I learned in this book to help with my anxiety?
- ☐ Did I lose my temper today?
- ☐ Did I use any of the tools in the book to control my anger?
- ☐ Did I say something nice to my friends today?
- ☐ Did I say something nice to my family today?
- ☐ Did I stick to my schedule?
- ☐ Did I eat healthily today?
- ☐ Did I get more than 8 hours of sleep last night?
- ☐ Have I worked on my physical health today?
- ☐ Have I worked on my mental health today?
- ☐ Have I worked on my social needs today?
- ☐ Have I worked on my spiritual needs today?

- ☐ Did I write down anything in my journal today?
- ☐ Have I done anything today to reach the goals on my vision board?
- ☐ Have I worked on addressing any bad habits today?
- ☐ Have I done any mindfulness exercises today?
- ☐ Have I conquered any fears today?
- ☐ Did I have fun today?
- ☐ Was today a good day or a bad day?
- ☐ Did I talk to myself in a positive way today?
- ☐ Have I spent time in nature or outside today?
- ☐ Have I done any physical activities today?

Thank You

Thank you so much for completing all the activities in this book! You are now one step closer to becoming the best version of yourself that can change the world! Remember that you are valuable and that it is important to love and care for yourself. Continue working hard through these exercises because these can be applied throughout your life. Thank you for caring enough about yourself to put in the work that can help you achieve your goals and dreams.

When you look in the mirror, you should also be grateful that you are committed enough to complete the project of working on yourself. With the help of these activities, all your mental, physical, and emotional needs will be fulfilled. Say, *thank you* to the person who bought this book for you. They care about you very much and have started you on an exciting adventure of self-discovery.

Part 2: CBT Toolbox for Teens

101 Exercises for Adolescents to Beat Anxiety, Manage Stress, and Boost Mental Well-Being

Letter to the Parent

Dear Parent,

Talking with teenagers can sometimes be challenging because they feel that their parents don't understand their struggles. They are also in a critical age where they are neither kids nor grownups. They don't want to ask for help, but they also can't handle certain things by themselves. Show your child that you understand what they are going through by giving them this book. It will give them the independence they need to tackle their issues while keeping you involved to provide guidance and assistance.

Your teenager can learn to control their thoughts, emotions, and behavior through the power of cognitive-behavioral therapy or CBT. Understandably, this is a new concept for your child. For this reason, the book introduces it in detail while highlighting how it manages intense emotions like phobias, anger, and anxiety.

Once your child grasps what CBT is and what it can do for them, they can learn certain aspects about themselves, like the relationship between their thoughts, emotions, and behavior and how each one can influence the other. This is significant information they should understand before they begin to apply CBT to their lives.

One of the main reasons you have probably decided to give your child this book is to help them with their anxiety. Anxiety is common among teens, but many don't recognize what they are going through or how it impacts their lives. The book explains this concept in detail with its symptoms and factors. Sometimes anxiety can be crippling, and your child can feel there is no escape from these emotions. However, the book manages to give them a glimmer of hope, letting them now that they aren't alone and that they can overcome it with CBT.

Fear is another issue that your child is struggling with and doesn't know what to do about it. As a parent, you understand how this emotion can be damaging to their self-esteem. Often, fear is irrational and stems from negative thoughts. Your child will learn here about their fears and how they can face and defeat them.

Negative thoughts change the way people see themselves and the world around them. You have probably experienced them firsthand; who hasn't? All parents wish they could protect their children from these thoughts so they could only see the good things in life. Similar to fear, negative thoughts can also be irrational. Your child will learn here how these thoughts affect them and how they are only focusing on the negatives while ignoring the positives.

It is heartbreaking watching your child going through depression. Since it is a sensitive issue, it can be tough to discuss it with them. Although this book isn't by any means a substitute for a therapist, it explains in a calm and friendly tone the concept of depression and its symptoms. It is necessary for your child to understand if they are depressed or just sad. Knowing the difference will give them a better understanding of what they are experiencing.

Anger has always been associated with teenagers. You have probably heard from family or friends that "Teens are angry all the time; it isn't just you." While anger is a natural emotion, it isn't normal for a person to be "angry all the time." The book explains to your child that the negative emotions they may be experiencing are the result of their anger. They will also learn about triggers so they can get to the root of their anger issues and control their explosive emotions.

Low self-esteem is another common issue among many teenagers. They can't help but compare themselves to many people their age. One can't forget the unrealistic beauty standards set by social media. Your child will learn how to change their thoughts so they can see themselves in a better light.

Do you remember when you were a teenager and had to do the things because you should rather than the things you want? People live according to certain rules, and sometimes, they forget to do what they love and enjoy. Your child needs to learn the stressful impact of all the "shoulds," identify their values, and change how they view these rules.

Don't you wish your teen was calm and at peace? This isn't impossible. There are certain strategies that they can implement that will make them feel relaxed and quiet their angry and negative thoughts.

Each chapter has a variety of fun and practical exercises and techniques based on Cognitive Behavioral Therapy (CBT) to empower teens. This book has all the information your child needs to begin their healing journey. It will be their guide every step of the way, and you will start to notice its impact on them.

However, this book is not a substitute for professional help. You must seek guidance from mental health professionals if your teenagers' challenges persist or worsen.

Letter to the Teenager

Hey there,

There is no denying that teenagers don't have it easy. More often than not, you feel alone and that no one understands you. You are under pressure at school and home and sometimes feel like you don't fit in anywhere. It's OK to feel this way, and you aren't alone. Your friends and many other teenagers feel this way, too. Your parents and your teachers did when they were your age. In fact, people of all ages experience stress and anxiety at some time in their lives.

Choosing to seek help is courageous and a step that will change your life. This book will be your guide and friend through this journey. It includes exercises and techniques that are fun and effective. They will change the way you think and feel about many things in life and provide you with methods to manage your stress, anxiety, and depression.

You are stronger than you think and have the power to change your life. Everything in life is a choice, even healing and positive changes. Making the decision to be and do better is brave. Take the first step today and get ready to meet a new you when you finish this book.

Section 1: How Can CBT Help Me?

CBT, or Cognitive Behavioral Therapy, is a type of talking therapy that includes many strategies, coping skills, and exercises to treat anxiety, depression, anger, grief, fears, and other issues. It focuses on the relationship between your thoughts, attitudes, and beliefs – and how they affect your actions and emotions.

In other words, your thoughts determine how you will feel and react in every situation. For instance, you and your teammates lost a big soccer match. This is upsetting. However, if you only focus on the loss, you will be disappointed and angry at yourself and your teammates. If you focus on how hard you and your teammates played and gave it your all, you will see it as an opportunity to learn from your mistakes and do better next time. This way, you will feel sad about the loss but won't be angry, and you're more likely to learn from your mistakes with this attitude; an angry attitude hinders your motivation.

CBT helps you develop better ways to deal with negative emotions.
https://www.pexels.com/photo/silver-iphone-6-987585/

CBT makes you aware of your negative thoughts or behavior towards a situation so you can develop different and better ways to behave and think. For instance, if you have a phobia of closed spaces, CBT can make you change the way you think and feel about them. Instead of being afraid, CBT will teach you how to change your perspective and that there is nothing scary about closed spaces, so you can feel safe and relaxed.

Benefits and Goals of CBT

- It provides results in a short amount of time.
- You don't need a therapist; you can practice these techniques alone at home.
- It treats a variety of intense emotions and negative behaviors.
- It teaches you to recognize and take control of unhelpful thoughts and change them to positive ones.
- You will also learn to think logically and realistically to challenge irrational negative thoughts.
- It boosts your self-esteem.
- You will learn problem-solving skills.
- It teaches you to identify and manage intense emotions.
- It provides you with coping skills to manage stress and anxiety.
- It teaches you to cope with grief and loss.
- It reduces your stress and teaches you different ways to relax and unwind.
- It teaches you to control your anger and healthily express your emotions.
- It treats depression and changes your behavior to a happy and upbeat person.
- It is one of the most common treatments against many types of anxiety, like phobias and social anxiety. You will learn how to challenge the thoughts making you anxious and face your fears. These techniques will show that your thoughts and fears aren't as bad or scary as you think.
- The skills you learn will benefit you for the rest of your life.
- It shows you that you can change and get better as soon as you believe you can.

Does CBT Work?

You are probably thinking, "This is too good to be true; does it actually work?" The short answer is yes, it does. Many children, teens, and adults swear by this technique.

Jessica, 12

Jessica was a happy girl who worked hard in school and always got good grades. However, when her parents divorced, she started acting out at home and school. Her parents took her to a therapist, and she told him that she was angry at her mom and dad for getting a divorce and destroying her family. The therapist used CBT techniques to change how Jessica thought of her parent's divorce. He showed her that they still loved her and are much happier now. He also taught her to recognize her negative thoughts and healthily express her feelings. After three months, she stopped acting out, accepted her parent's divorce, and went back to her old self.

Questions to Reflect on

1. Do I have negative thoughts?

2. What are these thoughts about?

3. Are my emotions out of control?

4. Am I ready to change my thoughts and manage my emotions?

Exercises

1. Journaling

Write down every negative thought or emotion you experienced throughout the day. Use smiley faces to describe how intense each one is.

2. Opinion or Fact

1. Think of your thoughts about yourself, like "My friends hate me" or "I won't get good grades."
2. In this worksheet, write which ones are facts and which are opinions. In other words, how realistic are your thoughts? Are you basing them on facts, or are they personal beliefs?

FACT OR OPINION

Facts are veri able statements. Opinions are personal interpretations of facts, which differ from person to person. For example, it is a fact that the sky is blue, and an opinion that the weather is beautiful.

Despite knowing the difference between facts and opinions, your brain does not always differentiate between the two. Harmful opinions, such as "I'm a bad person," are sometimes treated as fact. Even without evidence, these opinions may contribute to negative thinking, stress, and other problems.

Instructions: With practice, you can get better at spotting the difference between fact and opinion. Read each of the statements below and identify if they are fact or opinion

	Statement	Fact	Opinion
1.	I listened to my friend talk about their bad day.		
2.	I am a good friend.		
3.	I am ugly.		
4.	I have a blemish on my face.		
5.	My hair looks bad.		
6.	My boss said that I did a great job on the project.		
7.	No one will ever like me.		
8.	My crush said "no" when I asked them out.		
9.	I'm not as smart as the rest of my class.		
10.	I'm lazy.		
11.	I watched TV instead of doing my homework.		
12.	My friend is angry at me. I know this because they were frowning.		
13.	My friend frowned.		
14.	Everyone was bored during my speech.		
15.	I should always be nice.		

3. Worrying vs. Reality

Similar to the previous exercise, think of everything you are worried about and ask yourself, how likely are these things to happen? Write the most likely scenarios under reality and the least likely ones under worrying in the worksheet.

What Could Happen vs. What Will Happen

"When anxiety takes hold, it's often effortless to envision the most dire scenarios imaginable. However, it's crucial to recognize that these apprehensions may never materialize. The realm of possibility isn't synonymous with certainty."

What is something you are worried about?

Thinking about what will happen, instead of what could happen, can help you worry less. Whenever you start to worry, answer these questions:

What are some clues that your worry will not come true?

If your worry does not come true, what will probably happen instead?

If your worry does come true, how will you handle it? Will you eventually be okay?

After answering these questions, how has your worry changed?

----

4. Core Beliefs

Write down all your core beliefs about yourself, family, friends, school, and the world around you. You need to discover your beliefs to prepare yourself for the coming chapters.

5. Pros and Cons

Write down a particularly negative thought or belief you can't get out of your head in this worksheet, then write the pros and cons of having these thoughts/beliefs.

CBT Pros and Cons Worksheet

1. Choose the thought that you want to change

---

2. List the costs and benefits of the thought or behavior.

Costs	Benefits

3. After reviewing the costs and benefits of the current thought or behavior, develop a more adaptive alternative.

---

6. Catching the Negative Thoughts

Ask your friends and family what they really think of you and write it down. Next, read them out loud and see which of their opinions contradict your negative thoughts.

7. Problem-Solving Skills

Write down one of your biggest problems and come up with three solutions for it.

The Problem

The Solutions

1.

2.

3.

8. Negative Thoughts

Write down three situations where your negative thoughts held you back in life, and next to each one, write what you wish you had done differently.

1.

2.

3.

9. Negative Feelings

In this worksheet, write down some of your negative feelings like anger and stress, then write the consequences of each one, whether something that had already happened, like yelling at your siblings when you are angry, or what you imagine would happen. Then, write how you wish you would have handled the situation differently.

CHALLENGING NEGATIVE THOUGHTS

Depression, poor self-esteem, and anxiety are often the result of irrational negative thoughts. Someone who regularly receives positive feedback at work might feel that they are horrible at their job because of one criticism. Their irrational thought about job performance will dictate how they feel about themselves. Challenging irrational thoughts can help us change them.

Answer the following questions to assess your thought:

✱ Is there substantial evidence for my thought?

_____
_____

✱ Is there evidence contrary to my thought?

_____
_____

✱ Am I attempting to interpret this situation without all the evidence?

_____
_____

✱ What would a friend think about this situation?

_____
_____

✱ If I look at the situation positively, how is it different?

_____
_____

✱ Will this matter a year from now? How about five years from now?

_____
_____

10. Check in on Yourself

After exposing yourself to your negative emotions and thoughts, pause for a couple of minutes and check in on yourself. Write down how you are feeling mentally, emotionally, and physically.

_____

_____

_____

Section 2: Thoughts, Emotions, and Behaviors

The Cognitive Triangle

The cognitive triangle shows how thoughts, emotions, and behaviors affect one another. This means changing your thoughts will change how you feel and behave.

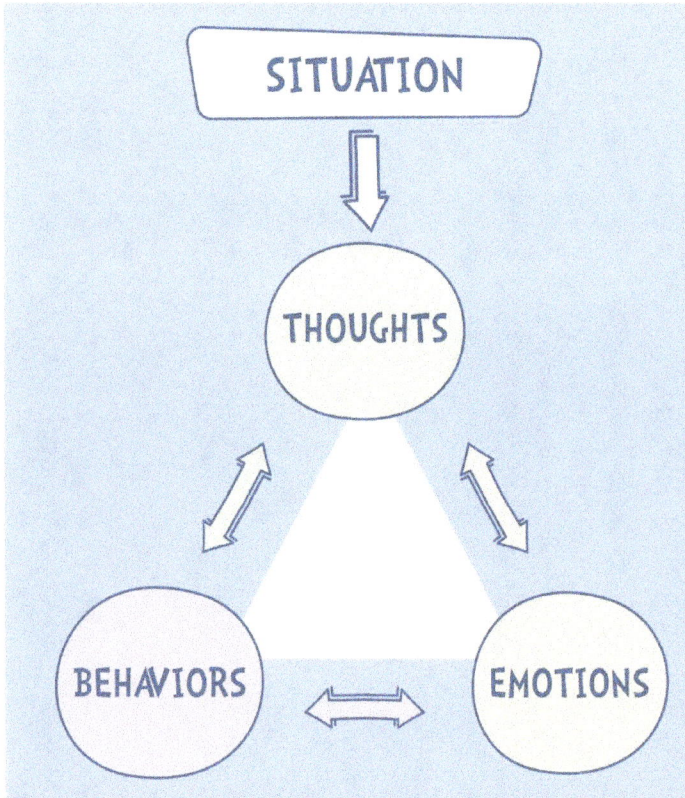

A SITUATION is anything that happens in your life, which triggers the cognitive triangle.

THOUGHTS are your interpretations of a situation. For example, if a stranger looks at you with an angry expression, you could think: "Oh no, what did I do wrong?" or "Maybe they are having a bad day."

EMOTIONS are feelings, such as happy, sad, angry, or worried. Emotions can have physical components as well as mental, such as low energy when feeling sad, or a stomachache when nervous.

BEHAVIORS are your response to a situation. Behaviors include actions such as saying something or doing something (or, choosing not to do something).

The cognitive triangle is a diagram that illustrates the relationship between your behavior, emotions, and thoughts.

Understanding Your Emotions

Behavior

Behavior reflects your actions in every situation. You change things, keep them the same, or make something happen. Your behavior can be external towards your surroundings or the people in your life, or internal through your feelings and thoughts.

Emotions

Emotions are how you feel about every situation you face in your life. For instance, you feel happy when you pass an exam, excited on your birthday, and sad when a loved one gets sick.

Thoughts

Thoughts are your beliefs and opinions about yourself, the world, and the people in your life. They can be positive or negative and can be so powerful that they change your personality. For instance, negative thoughts can make you angry and unhappy, while positive ones make you happy and upbeat.

Paying attention to your fleeting thoughts helps you understand and manage your emotions.
https://pxhere.com/en/photo/1189903

Your thoughts, emotions, and behavior are connected. Your emotions often reflect your thoughts, while both influence your behavior. For example, if you have negative thoughts about school, you will also develop negative emotions towards it and behave badly by acting out or not studying. Your emotions also affect your thoughts. If you feel sad or angry, you will have negative thoughts which will influence your behavior.

If you change one of them, the others will follow. For instance, if you have positive thoughts, you will feel happy and behave pleasantly.

"Thoughts create emotions, emotions create feelings, and feelings create behavior. So our thoughts must be positive to attract the right people, events, and circumstances into our lives." *Avis Williams.*

However, this isn't always easy, especially if you are consumed with automated thoughts. They are the negative and irrational beliefs you aren't aware of and can become your natural response to different situations. For example, you fail a test and react by thinking, *"I am a failure and will never amount to anything."*

These thoughts trigger negative emotions and make you feel scared, angry, anxious, sad, guilty, or ashamed. Naturally, these emotions will affect your behavior as well.

You should always pay attention to your emotional responses. Notice how every situation makes you feel. Are you sad, frustrated, irritated, or angry? Learning the names of different emotions is a great way to communicate how you feel.

Exercises

11. Venn Diagram

In this diagram, write down specific thoughts, emotions, and behaviors. Observe where they intersect, indicating the interdependence between these components.

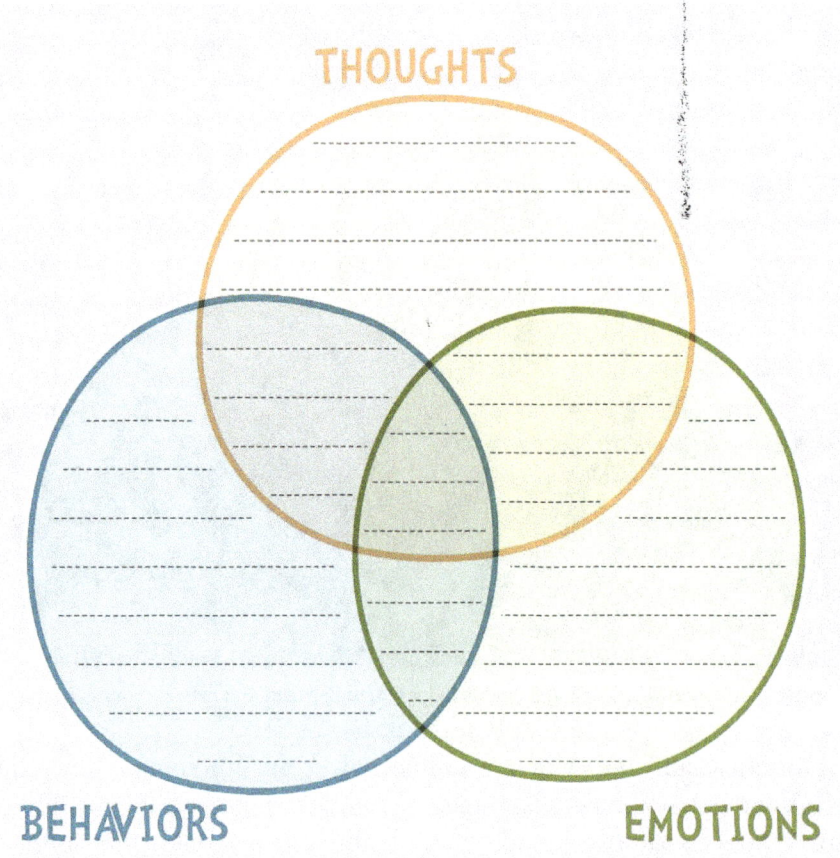

12. One Leads to Another

Write about an event or situation that triggered certain thoughts, emotions, and behaviors.

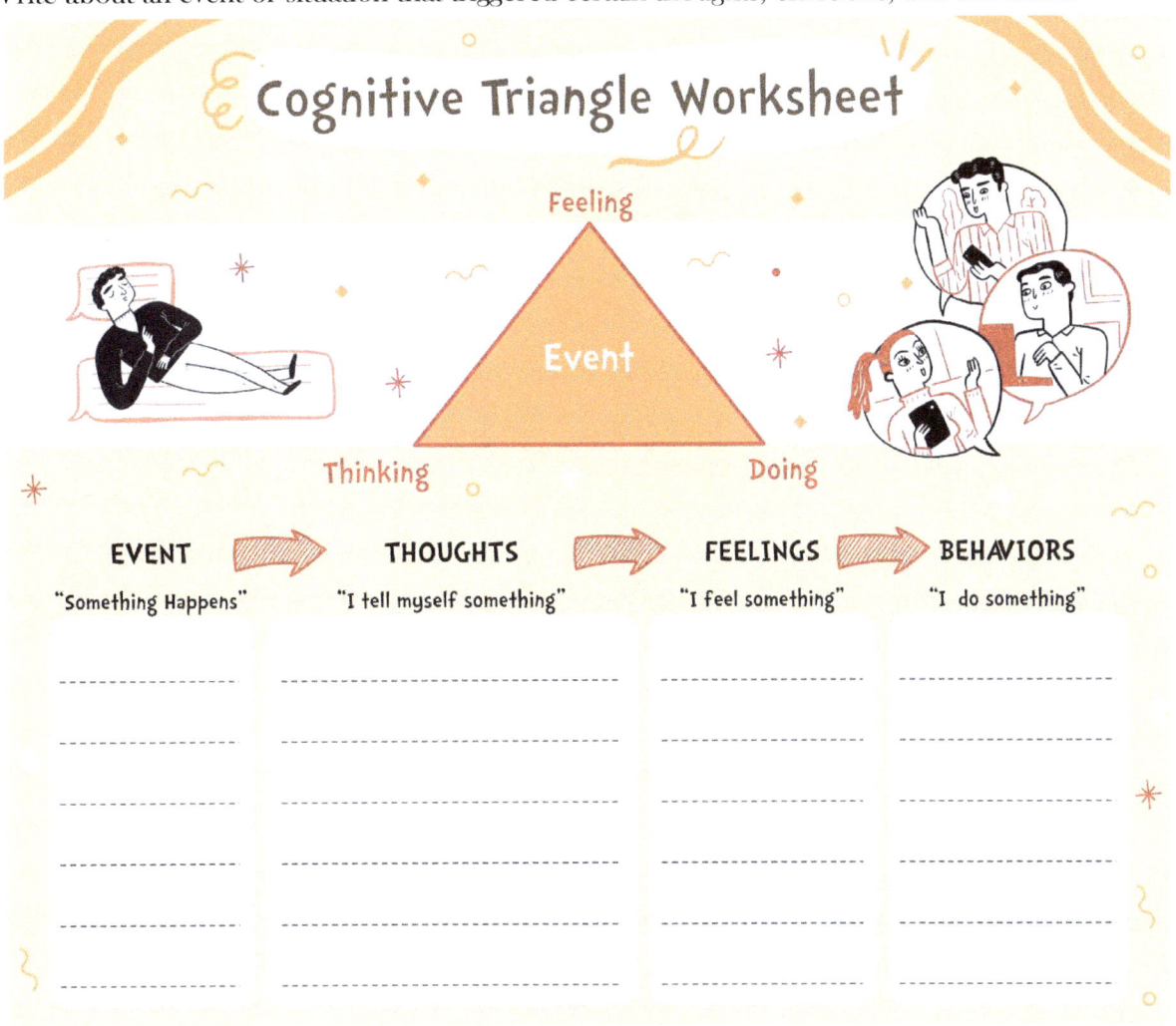

13. Emotional Vocabulary

Check the emotions in this worksheet and circle the ones you experienced in the last month.

List of Emotions

- Amazed
- Angry
- Annoyed
- Anxious
- Ashamed
- Bitter
- Bored
- Comfortable
- Confused
- Content
- Depressed
- Determined
- Disdain
- Disgusted
- Eager
- Embarrassed
- Energetic
- Envious
- Excited

- Foolish
- Frustrated
- Furious
- Grievous
- Happy
- Hopeful
- Hurt
- Inadequate
- Insecure
- Inspired
- Irritated
- Jealous
- Joy
- Lonely
- Lost
- Loving
- Miserable
- Motivated
- Nervous

- Overwhelmed
- Peaceful
- Proud
- Relieved
- Resentful
- Sad
- Satisfied
- Scared
- Self-conscious
- Shocked
- Silly
- Stupid
- Suspicious
- Tense
- Terrified
- Trapped
- Uncomfortable
- Worried
- Worthless

14. Recognize Automatic Thoughts

Fill this worksheet with different automatic thoughts you have experienced and their triggers, and replace them with new and positive ones.

For instance

- You didn't score in the last soccer game (Trigger)
- "My coach will kick me off the team because I am a failure." (Automatic thought)
- "I am a good player, and my coach knows it. I just made one mistake; he will understand." (New positive thought)

Our thoughts control how we feel about ourselves and the world around us. Positive thoughts lead to us feeling good and negative thoughts can put us down. Sometimes our thoughts happen so quickly that we fail to notice them, but they can still affect our mood. These are called automatic thoughts.

Oftentimes, our automatic thoughts are negative and irrational. Identifying these negative automatic thoughts and replacing them with new rational thoughts can improve our mood.

TRIGGER	AUTOMATIC THOUGHT	NEW THOUGHT
EXAMPLE: I made a mistake at work.	"I'm probably going to be fired. I always mess up. This is it. I'm no good at this job."	"I messed up, but mistakes happen. I'm going to work through this, like I always do."

15. Record Automatic Thoughts

Every time you experience an automatic thought like "I am going to fail this test," write it down. You should also include the situation, how these thoughts made you feel, and how you behaved.

16. Challenge These Thoughts

After you record your thoughts, write down why you think they are true and why they aren't. Read what you wrote aloud, then consider adding new positive thoughts to challenge the current ones.

17. Role-Play

Role-play various negative scenarios with your siblings, friends, or parents and notice the first thought that often comes to mind. They are most likely your automatic thoughts, so write them down to keep track of them.

Role-playing allows you to express different emotions and scenarios and their outcomes.
Julianne Zvalo-Martyn, CC BY-SA 4.0 <https://creativecommons.org/licenses/by-sa/4.0>, via Wikimedia Commons https://commons.wikimedia.org/wiki/File:Students_engaged_in_role_play.jpg

18. Cognitive Triangle

1. Inside the triangle, write down a tough situation you have been through lately.
2. Then, write your emotions, thoughts, and behavior during this situation.
3. Change your thoughts, emotions, or behavior to something positive. Write down how this will affect the other two and the situation's outcome.

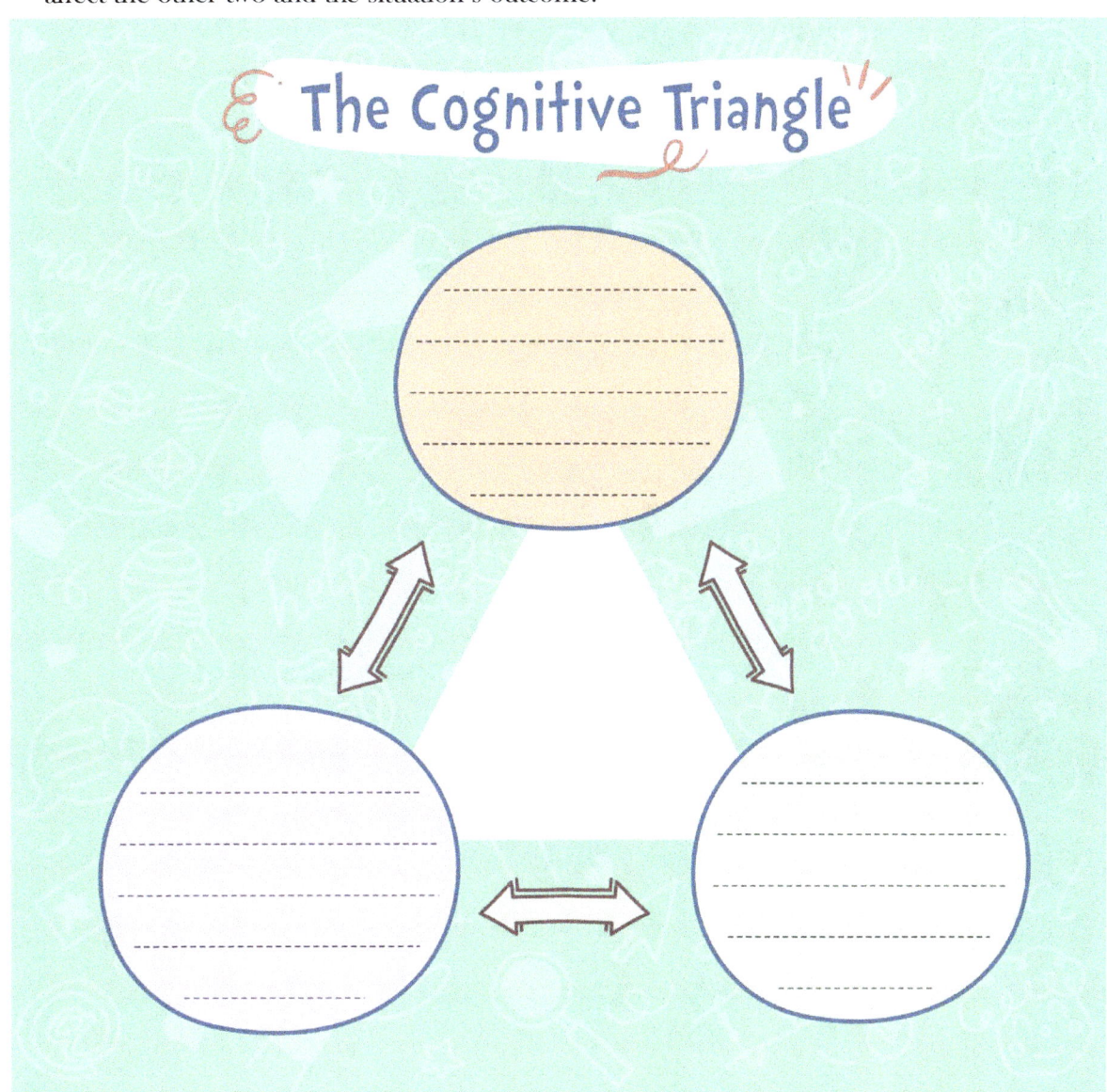

19. Thoughts Change

In this worksheet, write down a couple of situations that happened to you in the past and how they made you feel at the time. Now, reflect on these situations and write how you feel about them now compared to before. This exercise shows that you think differently with a clear head when time has passed, and your emotions have cooled down.

20. Emotional Charades

To better understand emotional responses, play emotional charades with your friends and family, where one acts a certain emotion and the other guesses it.

Section 3: Taming Anxiety

Anxiety is having a physical and mental reaction to various situations. If you have anxiety, you may not be aware of it. People use many words to describe this emotion, like feeling uneasy, on edge, worried, anguished, nervous, or having panic attacks. So, if you use any of these words to describe how you feel, you may suffer from anxiety.

Anxiety can creep up on you at any moment.
https://www.pexels.com/photo/photo-of-a-woman-crouching-while-her-hands-are-on-her-head-5542968/

Causes of Anxiety

- Stress
- Abuse
- Being bullied
- Trauma
- Loneliness and isolation
- Losing a loved one
- Constantly worrying about things that you have no control over, like earthquakes
- Pressure in school
- Seeing your parents going through financial problems or losing their jobs

Symptoms of Anxiety

- Uncontrollable worry
- Avoiding all anxiety triggers
- Having stomach problems
- Inability to sleep
- Only focusing on what's making you worried and failing to think about anything else
- Trouble concentrating at school
- Exhaustion
- Trembling
- Sweating
- Rapid breathing
- Fast heartbeat
- Panic attacks
- Feeling tense and nervous

There are certain thoughts, behaviors, and situations that escalate your anxiety. CBT reveals them to you so you can unmask specific patterns and triggers.

An Example of Using CBT to Overcome Anxiety

Justin struggled with anxiety all his life. He felt there was a war going on inside his head, and he couldn't quiet these thoughts. He tried CBT and breathing exercises whenever his thoughts were overwhelming. In time, he learned to cope with his anxiety and calm himself down.

Exercises

21. Track Your Pattern

To learn about your anxiety triggers, keep track of all "What if scenarios," intense emotions, and your behavior. You can carry a notebook, write them down immediately, and reflect on them at the end of the day to understand your anxiety pattern.

22. NO

Each time your mind wanders to negative "What-if scenarios," say out loud or under your breath, "No" or "Stop." This will interrupt the thought and bring you back to reality. Or you can use the "Shhh" technique like Captain America; Chris Evans once said, *"'Shhh' has been a big thing for me. It's so funny how noisy my brain is—and everyone's brain is noisy because that's what it does; it makes thoughts."*

Saying "No" can interrupt negative thoughts.

https://www.pexels.com/photo/person-holding-an-alphabet-4439408/

23. Feelings Change

1. Remember that feelings of anxiety won't last forever. So whenever you feel anxious, write down, "I am really worried right now, but it's OK. These feelings will go away, and I will feel calmer."
2. Now, imagine how you will feel when your emotions change, and write that down.

24. Act Normal

Whenever you experience anxiety in a non-threatening situation, let your anxiety know that you don't need it now by acting normally.

- Take deep breaths
- Have an open posture
- Smile

- Speak calmly

This way, your body lets your mind know there is nothing to worry about, and it should be relaxed. You can also chew gum since people don't do this when they are under threat.

25. Follow Your Train of Thought

Whenever you feel anxious about a situation, follow your train of thought. For example:

I don't want to speak up in class.

Why?

Because I am afraid people will laugh at me.

What will happen if they laugh at me?

This will hurt my feelings.

Have my classmates ever laughed at me before?

No.

So why would they laugh this time?

By following the train of thought, you can challenge it and prove it isn't based on anything real.

26. Repeat Affirmations

- This feeling will pass, and I will feel great again
- I can overcome my anxiety
- I am in control of my emotions
- I am capable and strong
- I trust myself

27. Breathing Exercise for Panic Attacks

Instructions:

1. Take a deep breath through your nostrils and fill your stomach with air.
2. Open your mouth and stick your tongue out.
3. Breathe out while roaring like a lion, or just say, "Ahh."
4. Repeat until you calm down.

28. 4-4-4-4 Breathing Exercise for Panic Attacks

Instructions:

1. Take a long, deep breath through your nostrils while counting to four.
2. Hold it and count to four.
3. Gently breathe out while counting to four.
4. Then pause and count to four.
5. Repeat until you feel calm.

29. Reframing Thoughts

Anxiety focuses on negative "What-if" scenarios. You can reframe these thoughts; instead of asking, "What if things go wrong?" try, "What if they went well?" For instance, you are worried about a test and keep thinking, "What if I fail?" "What if the test is hard?" "What if I panic and can't answer?" Adjust your thoughts by asking the opposite of these questions: "What if I pass?" What if the test is easy?" "What if I'm relaxed and answer all the questions?"

This technique allows you to interrupt negative thoughts with helpful ones that you can use to manage your anxiety.

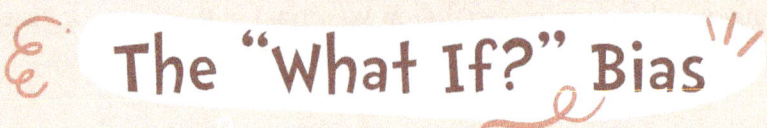

The "What If?" Bias

We often get caught up thinking about all the potential bad outcomes of a situation or decision, rather than adopting a rational perspective. This exercise can help you combat the "What If?" Bias to regain a balanced perspective and avoid catastrophizing.

Thinking of a situation or challenge that you'd like to tackle, use this worksheet to list both positive and negative "What Ifs?" in each of the columns.

Two examples are provided to get you started.

"What If" It's Negative?	"What If?" It's Positive?
E.g. What if I have a panic attack on stage?	E.g. What if I give the performance of my life?

30. Subjective Units of Distress Scale

Think of the last time you experienced anxiety and rate it from one to ten. Then, write in the empty spaces what triggered your anxiety and how to cope with this feeling.

Subjective Units of Distress Scale (SUDS)

Feelings of distress are subjective, meaning the experience of distress is influenced by personal feelings, tastes, or opinions. As such, we need a method to communicate with one another how much distress you're experiencing. The subjective units of distress scale (referred to as "SUDS") facilitate this communication as each individual anchors the scale with their own past experiences. Use the worksheet below to create your own SUDS. For each of the levels on the scale below, think of a time when you felt that degree of distress or anxiety. Since your experience of distress/anxiety may shift as you continue through treatment, it is best to anchor these levels on the scale with specific past events when you felt that way.

100 : Highest distress/anxiety that you've ever felt or could imagine feeling.
I was at a 100 when...
_____
_____

75 : Marked distress/anxiety; difficult to concentrate on anything else
I was at a 75 when...
_____
_____

50 : Moderate distress/anxiety
I was at a 50 when...
_____
_____

25 : Mild distress/anxiety; easy to shift attention away
I was at a 25 when...
_____
_____

0 : No distress/anxiety; relaxed
I was at a 0 when...
_____
_____

Questions

1. Write down a situation that often triggers your anxiety.

   _____

   _____

2. What is the worst outcome of this situation?

   _____

   _____

3. What is the most likely outcome?

   _____

   _____

4. What is the best outcome?

   _____

   _____

5. If the worst outcome happens, would it matter a year from now?

   _____

   _____

Section 4: Facing My Fear

Fear is a natural emotion when someone or something threatens you. Some fears are rational and real, like the fear of fire, while others are only in your head or imagination, like fearing that your classmates will laugh at you if you speak up in class. Since it isn't pleasant, many people think that fear is a negative emotion. However, it can be necessary to protect you from danger. For example, if you are scared of fire, you will never put your hand in it. On the other hand, if your fears are irrational and hold you back in life, they aren't healthy.

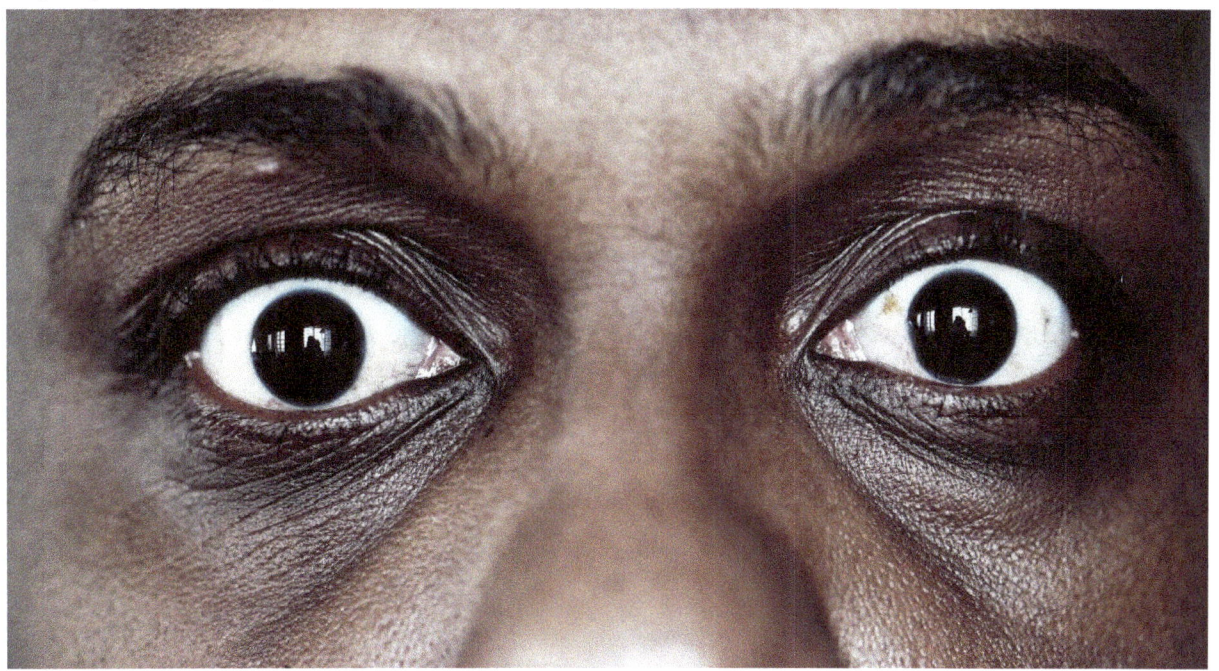

Fears can hold you back.

Fear and phobias can trigger your anxiety and make it hard for you to carry out daily activities.

"Everything you ever wanted is on the other side of fear." George Addair.

Causes of Fear

- Bad childhood memories like getting bitten by a dog or almost drowning
- Dangerous situations that can occur when walking alone at night
- Fear of uncertain situations like fear of the future
- Fears you have learned from the grownups in your life. For example, if your mom is afraid of cats and does not manage that fear around you, she might pass that fear on to you

Symptoms of Fear

- Upset stomach
- Shaking
- Sweating
- Shortness of breath
- Fast heartbeat
- Nausea
- Dry mouth
- Chills
- Chest pain

Fear vs. Worry vs. Phobia

You choose to be worried, but no one chooses fear. Fear is usually based on something real, a natural reaction to danger, while worry is usually in your head, like things you imagine will happen or things that come from your memory. In other words, you make up things in your head to worry about, but fear is out of your control and can be beneficial when it warns you of danger.

A phobia is different from fear and worry because it is an irrational fear of something that isn't dangerous. For example, spiders aren't threatening, yet many people fear them. A phobia is one of the main triggers of anxiety.

Phobia Triggers

- Genetics: if one of your parents has a phobia, you may have one, too
- Learned behavior: if you see your parents afraid of something, you will believe it's scary and develop the same phobia
- Bad experiences with an animal, situation, or place can trigger phobias
- Intense anxiety can also trigger phobias

Worry Triggers

- Unhealthy food
- Technology
- Peer pressure

- Hormonal changes
- Sleep deprivation

An Example of Using CBT to Overcome Fear

Rachel wanted to be an actress, but her stage fright held her back. She thought many times to participate in school plays, but just the thought gave her a stomachache. She tried gradual exposure, where she faced her fear step by step. She started by performing in front of the mirror, then she imagined she was performing in front of an audience. She then began performing in front of her siblings, then friends, then large family members. When she felt comfortable, she started taking small roles in plays until she felt ready to take bigger ones.

Exercises

31. Gradual Exposure

Instructions:

1. Write in this worksheet what your biggest fear is.
2. Starting from the bottom of the ladder, write each step you will take to gradually expose yourself to your fears.
3. The thought of facing your fear may cause you anxiety. It's OK; just take it one step at a time.

For example, if you are afraid of dogs, take these steps:

1. Watch pictures of dogs online.
2. Watch movies with dogs.
3. Be in the same room as a dog with adult supervision, and with the dog on a leash.
4. When you feel comfortable, you can slowly pet the dog while it's still on a leash.
5. When you are ready, remove the leash and play together.

Don't let your fear stop you; push through the anxiety with deep breaths. However, if your feelings are overwhelming or you experience a panic attack, it's time to take a step back and get yourself in a calm mental state. Take your time with each step, and don't move to the next one until you feel comfortable. Reward yourself every time you make progress.

Subjective Units of Distress Scale (SUDS)

To overcome our fears it can help to build our confidence gradually. You can think of it as being like climbing the steps of a ladder.
Start by writing down the fear that you are facing. Then for each step of the ladder write down one thing you can do to face that fear head-on. Make sure to reward yourself for each step you take

The fear I am facing is: _____

Most difficult

_____
_____
_____
_____
_____
_____
_____
_____
_____
_____
_____

Less difficult

32. Problem-Solving Skills

Instructions:

1. Write in the worksheet one of your fears.
2. Write down all the different ways you can cope with your fear. For example, if you are afraid of talking to new people, you can try taking a few deep breaths beforehand or start making small talk with salespeople.
3. Consider the advantages and disadvantages of each solution and write them down.
4. Choose the best solution and try it.
5. If it doesn't work, find another solution from the list.

You can use this technique with any problem, not just your fears.

PROBLEM SOLVING

 **Define Your Problem**

Before you define a problem, it might feel vague or confusing. Writing out your problem will help to organize information, see it from new angles, and identify the most important issues.

When and where does your problem occur?

What are the causes of your problem?
Think about all the possible causes. Consider your own behavior, as well as external factors.

Define your problem.
Be as clear and comprehensive as possible. If there are many parts to your problem, describe each of them.

TIP: If you find it difficult to separate your emotions from the problem, try to complete this step from the perspective of an impartial friend.

PROBLEM SOLVING

2 Develop Multiple Solutions

Write down at least three solutions to your problem. Without thinking about alternative solutions, we often get stuck on what worked in the past, or the first idea that comes to mind. There are usually many solutions to a problem, and our first ideas aren't always the best.

PROBLEM SOLVING

 **Assess Your Solutions and Choose One**

Begin by throwing out any solutions that are obviously ineffective or impractical. Next, look at your remaining solutions, and determine which ones are the most likely to be successful by examining them in-depth. This can be done by examining the strengths and weaknesses of each solution.

During this stage, you might come up with new solutions, or find that a combination of multiple solutions is better than any one idea.

Solution	Strengths	Weaknesses

TIP: If you're having a hard time thinking of strengths and weaknesses for each solution, ask yourself these questions:

- Is this a short-term or long-term solution?
- How likely am I to follow through with this solution?
- How will this solution affect other people?

PROBLEM SOLVING

 **4** Implement Your Solution

To ensure you follow through with your solution, it's best to think of how and when it will be implemented. Without doing so, solutions that are difficult might be avoided, or they can slip your mind when the time comes.

When will you implement your solution?

Some solutions can happen at a specific time (e.g. "2:00 PM on Saturday"), while others require something unpredictable to happen (e.g. "when I get angry"). Fill in the relevant section below:

My solution can be scheduled...

When will you implement your solution? Be specific.

How will you remember to follow through with your solution?

My solution is in response to something...

How will you know when to use your solution?
List specific warning signs, triggers, or other specific events that will tip you off.

List the specific steps you will take to implement your solution.

TIP: If your solution requires a lot of time or effort, try to break the process into small steps. It's easier to follow through with several small steps, rather than one giant task.

PROBLEM SOLVING

5 Review

Finally, after implementing your solution, you will review what worked and what didn't. Even if your problem was a one-time situation, there are often broader lessons to be learned. Take a moment to reflect on your problem and how you handled it.

In what ways was your solution effective?

In what ways was your solution not effective?

If you could go back in time, what would you change about how you handled the problem?

What advice would you give to someone else who was dealing with the same problem?

---

33. Overcoming Safety Behavior

Safety behavior is avoiding your fears to protect yourself. However, this is a temporary solution that can only make your anxiety worse.

Instructions:
1. Ask yourself how often you avoid your fear or anxiety triggers.
2. Write down all the different ways you avoid them, like ordering everything online because making small talk makes you nervous or sitting in the back of the classroom to avoid attention.
3. You can then slowly and gradually do the opposite of each situation, like sitting in the middle of the classroom or ordering food on the phone.
4. Consider the gradual exposure technique, as it helps you make progress at your own pace.

34. Breathing Technique

Instructions:
1. Take a deep and long breath into your abdomen.
2. Breathe out from your mouth.
3. Take another deep breath from your nostrils and notice your belly rising.
4. Close your eyes and imagine the air flowing through your body.
5. Breathe out and release the air from your body.
6. Repeat until you calm down.

35. Art Work

Art is a great way to reduce and cope with fears, worries, and anxiety. Whenever you feel any of these emotions, draw or doodle anything. If you don't like drawing, try coloring books. You can also try other art forms to get you out of your head, like dancing, singing, and writing.

36. Yoga

Yoga is very relaxing and an effective coping skill.

Child's pose.
Iveto, CC BY-SA 4.0 <https://creativecommons.org/licenses/by-sa/4.0>, via Wikimedia Commons: https://commons.wikimedia.org/wiki/File:Balasana.JPG

Instructions:
1. Find a quiet spot at home with no distractions.
2. Sit on the yoga mat, just like the picture.
3. Remain in this position for five minutes.
4. Clear your mind and breathe into your belly.
5. Remain focused, and bring your mind back to the present moment whenever it wanders.

37. Relaxing Meditation

Instructions:
1. Sit in a quiet room in a comfortable position.
2. Close your eyes and take deep and slow breaths.
3. Focus on your breathing and nothing else.
4. If your mind wanders or thoughts creep into your head, don't give them attention and let them pass.

38. Draw Circles

Instructions:
1. Get crayons or pens of different colors and a notebook.
2. Draw circular patterns and keep focused on the drawing activity.
3. The patterns don't have to be pretty; it's the activity that matters.
4. Keep drawing for a few minutes, then change the pattern and the pen or crayon color.

39. Mental Contrasting

Mental contrasting is thinking positively about the future while acknowledging the hardships you might face to reduce your fear of the future.

Instructions:
1. Visualize making your biggest dreams come true or achieving all your goals.
2. Imagine how great your life would be and how you would feel.
3. Acknowledge the problems and hardships that could stand in your way, like lack of motivation.
4. Make a plan to overcome these obstacles.

40. Affirmations

- *I am supported, I am loved, and I am safe.*
- *I am releasing all my fears, worries, and stress.*
- *My mind is quiet and calm.*
- *I am letting go of any emotions that don't serve me.*
- *I treat myself with kindness.*

Section 5: Overcoming Mental Filtering

Mental filtering occurs when you only focus on the negative aspect of a situation and filter out or ignore the positive. In other words, your mind chooses to only see the bad side of life (even if it is small) and refuses to see all the other good things that are happening around you.

For example, you got straight As in all subjects, but you got a C in the last math exam. You only focus on this one exam and tell yourself you are a failure and a bad student. You ignore all the praise you have received from your teachers and all your other good test results and judge yourself based on this one test.

Or your best friend does something to upset you but tries to apologize and make it up to you. However, you don't want to see all their efforts and are only focused on this one mistake.

Mental filtering keeps away the positive thoughts, as a water filter does with dirt, except it filters the good thoughts and leaves you with the bad ones. Understand that there are always good things around you and happy thoughts in your head. Your mind is just keeping them from you,

The Effect of Mental Filtering on Your Life

Mental filtering can help you see the good side of every situation.
https://www.pexels.com/photo/woman-holding-a-smiley-balloon-1236678/

Mental filtering will change the way you view your reality. You will exaggerate the negatives, lower your self-esteem, and have a pessimistic opinion of yourself and the world. You will be blind to all the good things in your life and constantly feel like a failure even if you are accomplished. Eventually, you may fall into depression. Luckily, CBT techniques can do wonders for your thoughts and mental health.

An Example of Using CBT for Mental Filtering

Ryan struggled with seeing the good things in life. He always felt like someone had put a blindfold on his eyes when there was anything good happening around him. However, things started to change when he tried CBT. He used affirmations every day to remind himself that he is an awesome person and that his life is pretty great. The more he repeated words like "I am clever and good at what I do" or "I am lucky to have great family and friends," the more he believed them. So whenever something bad happened, these affirmations quickly challenged these negative thoughts to remind him that one mistake doesn't define him. Eventually, he started to focus more on the positives instead of the negatives.

Exercises

41. ABC Model

This exercise will make you aware of your negative thoughts and mental filtering tendencies so you can change and transform your way of thinking.

Instructions:

1. Write in the "A" in the worksheet an event that has happened recently that triggered negative thoughts.
2. Write in "B" your beliefs or understanding of the event. For example, you are close to one of your classmates, but they didn't invite you to their birthday party, so you believe they don't like you.
3. Write in "C" how the situation made you feel and affected your behavior. For example, you were sad or angry and decided not to talk to your classmate again.
4. In "D," create new beliefs or outcomes to the situation, like maybe they didn't invite you because it was a small party.
5. In "E," come up with new beliefs, like believing that your classmate likes you because they never acted otherwise, and there is probably a misunderstanding.

ABC Model

Activating Event
Something happens to you or in the environment around you.

Beliefs
You have a belief or interpretation regarding the activating event.

Consequences
Your belief has consequences that include feelings and behaviors.

Disputations of Beliefs
Challenge your beliefs to create new consequences.

Effective New Beliefs
Adoption and implementation of new adaptive beliefs.

42. Cognitive Restructuring

This technique can alter your thoughts so you can calmly express your emotions.

- Write down the negative thoughts.
- What evidence do you have that supports it, and what evidence is against it?
- Is this thought based on my emotions or facts?
- Can this thought be more flexible?
- Am I misunderstanding the evidence and just making assumptions?
- If I ask my parents and siblings about this situation, what will their thoughts be?
- Am I ignoring the evidence that doesn't support my thought?
- Am I exaggerating the truth?
- Is my negative thought an automatic response or based on facts?
- Did someone influence my thoughts? Are they trustworthy?
- Is this thought based on something real or a worst-case scenario?

43. Negative Thoughts vs. Positive Thoughts

Fill out the worksheet. This exercise will make you see the difference between your negative and positive thoughts to determine which ones are more rational.

Situation
Something happens. This step covers only the facts of what happened, without any interpretation.

	My Actual Thought	Alternate Thought

Thought
Using thought, you interpret the situation. These interpretations are not always accurate. There are many ways to think about the same situation.

Feeling
You experience emotions based upon your thoughts about the situation.

Behavior
You respond to the situation based upon your thoughts and feelings.

44. Decatastrophizing

Catastrophizing is when you exaggerate a situation in your head and focus on negative outcomes. Decatastrophizing challenges your negative thoughts and gives a realistic view of the situation.

Fill out the worksheet.

Decatastrophizing

Cognitive distortions are irrational thoughts that have the power to influence how you feel. Everyone has some cognitive distortions—they're a normal part of being human. However, when cognitive distortions are too plentiful or extreme, they can be harmful.

One common type of cognitive distortion is called catastrophizing. When catastrophizing, the importance of a problem is exaggerated, or the worst possible outcome is assumed to be true. By learning to question your own thoughts, you can correct many of these cognitive distortions.

What are you worried about?

How likely is it that your worry will come true? Give examples of past experiences, or other evidence, to support your answer.

If your worry does come true, what's the worst that could happen?

If your worry does come true, what's most likely to happen?

If your worry comes true, what are the chances you'll be okay...

In one week? _____%   In one month? _____%   In one year? _____%

45. Thoughts Trial

In this fun exercise, you will pretend one of your negative thoughts is on trial, and you are the judge, prosecutor, and lawyer. Fill out this worksheet and present the evidence that supports it and the evidence against it. After you finish, pass judgment based on the information you provided.

In this exercise, you will put a thought on trial by acting as a defense attorney, prosecutor, and judge, to determine the accuracy of the thought.

Prosecution and Defense:
Gather evidence in support of, and against, your thought. Evidence can only be used if it's a verifiable fact. No interpretations, guesses, or opinions!

Judge:
Come to a verdict regarding your thought. Is the thought accurate and fair? Are there other thoughts that could explain the facts?

THE THOUGHT

THE DEFENSE	THE PROSECUTION
evidence for the thought	evidence against the thought

THE JUDGE'S VERDICT

46. Challenge Your Inner Rules

People have negative or self-critical rules that affect how they see themselves or the world, like "If I fail a test, I am a failure." Fill out the worksheet to better understand your rules.

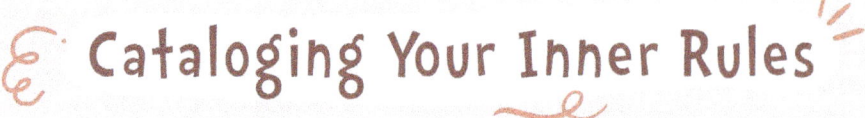

Cataloging Your Inner Rules

We all have rules that guide our behavior on a daily basis. We might not be able to clearly articulate all of them, but they hang around in our subconscious and nudge us towards behavior that is consistent with them. Many of these rules might be good (e.g., "Good people don't badmouth others behind their back") but some of them might not be adaptive or helpful (e.g., "If you make one mistake, you are a bad person").

Use this worksheet to help you identify a questionable or harmful rule you have and challenge it.

THE INFRACTION
What did you do that broke one of your internal rules?

THE RULE
What rule did your behavior break? Why did you feel bad after engaging in that behavior?

THE RULE'S ORIGINS
Where did it come from? What makes you think the rule is right, or a good rule?

ADVANTAGES OF KEEPING THIS RULE
How does this rule help you?

DISADVANTAGES OF KEEPING THIS RULE
How does this rule hurt you?

What to Do with This Rule: ☐ Keep It ☐ Trash It ☐ Modify It

THE RULE GOING FORWARD
What is the best possible version of this rule?

47. Challenge Negative Thoughts

Fill out this worksheet to learn to filter the negative thoughts instead of the positive ones.

48. Role Play

Think of a situation where you filtered positive thoughts. Then, you can mention all the negatives in the situation, and the other person will list the positives. Try to challenge each other with evidence like a lawyer and prosecutor.

49. Affirmations

- *I embrace love and positivity.*
- *I see all the obstacles disappearing from my life.*
- *Today is a good day full of joy and exciting opportunities.*

- *I solve my problems with positive thinking.*
- *I control my thoughts, and I only allow positivity in.*

Section 6: Beating The Blues

Everyone feels sad and even goes through depression at some time in their lives. A person can be laughing and having fun, but inside, they are fighting a battle that no one else knows about. There is no denying that these feelings are hard, and you might feel that no one can understand what you're going through. You aren't alone; sadness, pain, and depression are more common than you think.

Depression can make you feel helpless.
https://www.pexels.com/photo/woman-in-black-jacket-3209136/

In any superhero movie, the hero uses their pain as motivation to keep fighting; they don't allow it to hold them back, and neither should you. Once you understand what you're going through, you can find the right methods and help yourself get better. All the information and exercises in this book can aid in managing depression symptoms and treating the blues.

However, if these techniques don't work, understand that it's OK. There are other ways to get support. Ask a friend, family member, teacher, or someone you trust for help. How many people love you and want to see you feel better will surprise you.

What Is Depression?

Depression is feeling down and blue all the time, accompanied by losing interest in the activities you once enjoyed.

Causes of Depression

- Family history: if someone from your family suffers from depression, there is a possibility you will suffer from it.
- Some personality types are more prone to depression, such as those who suffer from anxiety, low self-esteem, and high sensitivity.
- Being bullied
- Early puberty
- Trauma
- Social media
- Pressure at school

Symptoms of Depression

- Anger
- Loss of energy
- Constantly feeling tired
- Ignoring your appearance and hygiene
- Isolating from family and friends
- Slow movements
- Noticeable weight gain or weight loss
- Sleeping too much or insomnia
- Feeling sad for no reason
- Pessimism or hopelessness
- Irritability
- Feeling guilty or worthless
- Self-criticism or self-blame

CBT is an effective tool for managing sadness and depression because it changes how you think, influencing your behavior and putting you in a good mood. Since sadness and depression are common among teenagers, many have used CBT techniques like thought reframing, meditation, and journaling to challenge their negative thoughts, change their thought patterns, and calm their nerves.

An Example of Someone Using CBT for Anger

Jack used to feel tired all the time and would sleep all day. He was always sad and hopeless, lost his appetite, and suffered anxiety. Jack tried journaling, behavior activation, and thought restructuring to bring his attention to the good things in his life. He also practiced meditation every day to reduce his anxiety.

Exercises

50. Mental Contrast for Depression
Instructions:
1. Imagine your worst-case scenario or fear coming true.
2. Imagine the consequences of this situation.
3. Think about all the tools you can use to prevent this scenario from coming true.
4. Make a plan to use all your resources to prevent it from happening.

51. Pleasant Activity Scheduling (PAS)

Fill this worksheet with the activities and responsibilities that you used to do before the depression to encourage you to go back to your old life. Rate how you feel.

Behavioral Activation

You can begin to decrease depression by engaging in activities you find enjoyable, and by taking care of responsibilities that you have been neglecting.

List three activities you enjoy:

1. _____
2. _____
3. _____

List three responsibilities you need to take care of:

1. _____
2. _____
3. _____

Try doing at least one activity or responsibility each day. Use the following scale to rate your depression, pleasant feelings, and sense of achievement before and after the activity.

```
0    1    2    3    4    5    6    7    8
None                Moderate              Extreme
```

Activity (location, date, time)		Depression	Pleasure	Achievement
	Before			
	After			
	Before			
	After			
	Before			
	After			

52. Black-and-White Thinking

Black-and-white thinking is believing things are bad or good with no middle ground. This exercise will teach you to let go of this type of thinking.

Black-and-white thinking often uses extreme words like always or never: "I will never succeed" or "I am always failing." Write down ten of your black-and-white thoughts in this worksheet and use words like "I am flexible enough to," "I am willing to," "I am noticing that," or "sometimes."

Black & White Thinking

Black and white thinking, also known as all-or-nothing thinking, is a cognitive distortion that involves seeing things in extreme categories, such as success or failure, good or bad, and right or wrong, without any shades of gray or nuance.

Examples of Black & White Thinking:

"I'm not good enough if I don't get the job."

"If a friend doesn't call me back within an hour, they don't care about me"

"I'm lazy if I don't exercise 5 days a week."

"I can't have both good grades and a social life."

"I'm weak if I can't stick to healthy eating 100% of the time."

Finding the 'Gray' Area:

Write down a black and white thought you had recently, that may not be 100% true all the time, or that is not based 100% on veri able fact. After that, write another perspective that is in the gray area.

Black & White Thought:

If a friend doesn't call me back within an hour, they don't care about me"

Re-framed Thought:

There are many other reasons my friend might not be able to call me back right now, and I don't know for sure if it relates to how much they care.

Black & White Thought:

Re-framed Thought:

Black & White Thinking

Black and white thinking, also known as all-or-nothing thinking, is a cognitive distortion that can cause harm in various aspects of life. It can lead to negative thoughts, self-sabotaging behaviors, and limit opportunities and progress.

How has black and white thinking affected your life?

Fill in the circle for any of the Black and White thinking consequences you have experienced, then write about your experience below.

○ Do my thoughts tend to cause misunderstandings and missed opportunities for compromise and resolution of conflicts in my relationships?

○ Does my fixed mindset prevent me from learning and achieving my full potential?

○ Do my thoughts limit opportunities and hinder collaboration and progress in the workplace?

○ Does my black and white thinking disrupt my healthy eating habits by creating rigid dietary restrictions and unhealthy relationships with food?

○ Do my thoughts lead to negative thoughts and emotions and self-sabotaging behaviors?

○ Do my thoughts cause me to make decisions without considering the impact on myself and others?

○ Do my thoughts lead me to idealize and devalue others, causing emotional upheaval in my relationships?

○ Do my thoughts lead me to make assumptions without verifying facts?

○ Do my thoughts filter out positive information and only focus on the negative?

○ Does my black and white thinking cause anxiety by exaggerating the probability of something negative happening?

How has black and white thinking affected you?

_____

_____

_____

Black & White Thinking

This worksheet will guide you through a series of questions to help you evaluate your thoughts and determine if they involve black and white thinking. Write down a thought you had recently, then check the boxes.

Write down the thought:

_____
_____
_____

YES   (May be Black and White Thinking)

○ Is the thought overly simplistic or extreme?

○ Does the thought involve rigid "should" or "must" statements?

○ Does the thought involve thinking in absolutes, such as "always" or "never"?

○ Is there no room for nuance or complexity in the thought?

○ Does the thought involve jumping to conclusions without considering all the evidence?

○ Are there other possible explanations or perspectives that the thought ignores?

○ Does the thought involve personalizing or globalizing an event?

○ Does the thought involve catastrophizing or minimizing the situation?

○ Does the thought involve discounting the positive or exaggerating the negative?

○ Does the thought involve focusing on one aspect of the situation and ignoring the others?

○ Does the thought involve making assumptions without verifying the facts?

○ Does the thought involve overgeneralizing from one negative experience?

Changing black and white thinking takes time to master, but with practice it will become second nature.

53. Overgeneralization

Overgeneralization is applying the same thought to multiple situations. For instance, if you lose one game, you tell yourself, "I never win any games." Try this exercise to challenge these thoughts.

1. Think of someone you love dearly, like your best friend or sibling.
2. Imagine they come to you with one of your overgeneralized thoughts like "I mess up every time I speak in class."
3. Write down three things you would tell them.

-
-
-

4. How different are they from your inner thoughts?

5. Would you tell your sibling the same things you tell yourself? If not, then why not?

6. Why don't you treat yourself with the same kindness?

54. Journaling

1. Write down in your notebook a catastrophizing (exaggerated) thought. This way, you will separate yourself from it and look at it as if it belongs to someone else.
2. When you read it a few times, you will realize that this thought is irrational.
3. You will start to think more objectively and come up with helpful thoughts.

55. Walking Meditation

1. Go for a walk while focusing on each step.
2. Notice how many breaths you take with every step and how fast you walk.
3. Focus on how your lungs feel with every breath.
4. Match your breathing with your steps.
5. Take a deep breath, count three steps, then breathe out and take three steps.
6. Feel the wind in your hair and focus on where you are and what you are doing.

56. Visualization

1. Sit in a quiet room in a comfortable position.
2. Close your eyes and take a few deep breaths.
3. Imagine you are in your favorite place.
4. You can see yourself happy and having fun.
5. Feel everything around you with your five senses to make the image as real as possible.
6. Stay in this place until you feel relaxed.

57. Breathing Exercise

1. Lie down and place one hand on your chest and the other on your stomach.
2. Take a deep breath through your nostrils and let your stomach push your hand out.
3. Breathe out through your lips as if you're whistling.
4. Repeat five times.

58. Label Your Thoughts

1. Close your eyes and take a deep breath.
2. Allow yourself to think of your negative thoughts.
3. Whenever you have a thought, label it as what it is: a "Thought." For example, say, "I am thinking that I am not a good friend."
4. Keep repeating to convince yourself that it's just a thought and not a fact.

59. Affirmations

- *I deserve more than what my mind tells me.*
- *I am enough.*
- *I am a good person.*
- *I find beauty in my broken parts.*
- *My mistakes don't define me.*

Section 7: Controlling Anger

Anger is a strong emotion that you feel when someone insults you or when something goes wrong. When expressed calmly, anger is a helpful feeling that lets others know you are upset or frustrated.

Expressing anger calmly can help people understand that you're frustrated.

https://unsplash.com/photos/sLrw_Cx6u_I?utm_source=unsplash&utm_medium=referral&utm_content=creditShareLink

Anger Triggers

- Feeling misunderstood or unheard
- Getting blamed for something you didn't do
- When someone makes fun of you
- Feeling threatened
- Mistreatment

- Stress
- The Effects of Anger on Your Health
- Increases your anxiety
- Depression
- Headaches
- Insomnia
- Skin issues
- Clouds your judgment
- Increases negative thoughts
- Stresses you out
- Isolation
- Low self-esteem
- Violent behavior

CBT will teach you how to control your emotions. These techniques can challenge the negative thoughts caused by anger and replace them with compassionate, helpful, and rational thoughts.

Exercises

60. SUDS Scale

Think of the last time you got angry and rate it from one to ten. Then, color the scale depending on how angry you currently feel. In separate sections, write down the triggers that commonly lead to your anger, and another section to note what you can do to control your anger effectively.

61. Cognitive Restructuring

Cognitive restructuring or cognitive reframing is a CBT method that makes you notice your negative thoughts and challenge them. You will eventually realize that these thoughts are either irrational or exaggerated in your head. You can then "reframe" them to start thinking positively.

Fill the worksheet just like in exercise number 43, but focus on thoughts that made you angry.

- Write down the negative thought.
- What evidence do you have that supports it, and what evidence is against it?
- Is this thought based on my emotions or facts?
- Can this thought be more flexible?
- Am I misunderstanding the evidence and just making assumptions?
- If I ask my parents and siblings about this situation, what will their thoughts be?
- Am I ignoring the evidence that doesn't support my thought?
- Am I exaggerating the truth?
- Is my negative thought an automatic response or based on facts?
- Did someone influence my thoughts? Are they trustworthy?
- Is this thought based on something real or a worst-case scenario?

62. Behavioral Experiment

Anger is usually based on irrational thoughts that intensify your emotions and make you lose your temper. This exercise will test the negative thoughts to see how they affect your behavior and mood. Just imagine a scenario with this thought and predict how you will react. Or you can experiment with it by thinking about this thought with your family and friends and seeing its effect on you.

Behavioral Experiment

Our thoughts and beliefs determine how we feel, and how we act, at any given moment. Even thoughts that are irrational impact our mood and behavior, often negatively. A behavioral experiment is a tool for testing our thoughts and beliefs, and replacing those that are irrational with healthy alternatives.

Part 1: Experiment Plan

Thought to Test
What is the thought or belief you would like to test?

Experiment
How can you test this thought?

When will you run the experiment?

Prediction
What do you think will happen during the experiment?

How do you expect to feel after the experiment?

○—○—○—○—○
VERY BAD · NEUTRAL · VERY GOOD

Part 2: Experiment Results

Outcome
What happened during the experiment?

How did you feel after the experiment?

○—○—○—○—○
VERY BAD · NEUTRAL · VERY GOOD

New Thought
Given the evidence from the experiment, what is your new thought?

63. Track Your Mood

Use this worksheet to track your mood for a week to identify negative thoughts.

Weekly Mood Chart

	Monday	Tuesday	Wednesday	Thursday	Friday	Saturday	Sunday
6 AM - 10 AM							
10 AM - 2 PM							
2 PM - 6 PM							
6 PM - 10 PM							
10 PM - 2 AM							
2 AM - 6 AM							

64. Daily Mood Chart

This exercise will track your emotions every day so you can monitor your angry behavior.

	Happy	Sad	Mad	Tired	Excited	Anxious	Other	Notes
6 AM - 8 AM								
8 AM - 10 AM								
10 AM - 12 PM								
12 PM - 2 PM								
2 PM - 4 PM								
4 PM - 6 PM								
6 PM - 8 PM								
8 PM - 10 PM								
10 PM - 12 AM								
12 AM - 2 AM								
2 AM - 4 AM								
4 AM - 6 AM								

65. Thought Log

Write an event that angered you, your negative thoughts, how they affected your behavior and actions, and how you wish you responded.

Event	Thought	Consequence (emotion & behavior)	Alternate Response

66. Anger Diary

Every night before you go to sleep, reflect on a person or situation that made you angry.

Anger Diary

EVENT THREE
- Trigger
- Warning Signs
- Anger Response
- Outcome

EVENT FOUR
- Trigger
- Warning Signs
- Anger Response
- Outcome

EVENT FIVE
- Trigger
- Warning Signs
- Anger Response
- Outcome

REVIEW
- Do you notice any patterns related to your anger?
- Generally, how would you like to react differently?

67. Meditation
Instructions:
1. Take a deep breath and focus on your feet.
2. Flex, move your toes, and imagine the anger leaving your body through your toes.
3. Next, focus on your legs and squeeze the muscles, then imagine the anger leaving your body from your legs.
4. Repeat the previous steps with your torso, neck, shoulders, arms, and face.

68. Breathing Exercise
Instructions:
1. Hold a flower and take a deep breath, taking in its scent.
2. Hold your breath while counting to three.
3. Breathe out through your mouth and count to four.
4. Repeat until you calm down.

69. Affirmations
- *I am in control of my anger.*
- *I choose to respond with kindness rather than anger.*
- *My heart and mind are free of anger and anxiety.*
- *I will never choose anger.*
- *I express myself with understanding and respect.*

Section 8: My Self-Esteem

Self-esteem is how you see and value yourself. It's your self-beliefs and your opinions about your looks, personality, character, and life. Low self-esteem is common among many teenagers who often question their identity and if they are good enough and compare themselves to their peers.

Being bullied can affect your self-esteem.
https://www.pexels.com/photo/a-student-getting-bullied-by-schoolmates-7396383/

Factors Influencing Your Self-Esteem

How many hours do you spend on social media? Your parents have probably told you many times to put the phone down, but you just can't. However, they have a point here. Social media can damage your self-esteem.

All the pictures you see online are either filtered or heavily edited. The "spontaneous" photos your favorite celebrities post of themselves are anything but spontaneous. It takes them hours to get the right lighting, makeup, and pose to make it look like it does. Even the "no makeup look" is a lie. No one posts a picture of themselves showing the dark lines under their eyes. They actually use makeup that looks natural. All these images can lower your self-esteem as you keep comparing yourself to these unrealistic beauty standards.

You also see people online posting about their vacations and having fun, and you feel your life is boring in comparison. Understand that nothing you see on social media is real. People only post about the good things in their lives. No one will post about crying themselves to sleep or having a broken heart.

Loneliness can also affect your self-esteem. Spending time alone with your negative thoughts can make you feel bad about yourself. You should be around people who lift you up and make you happy!

Exercises

70. Challenge the Thought

Whenever you have a negative thought that affects your self-esteem, ask yourself, "What is this thought costing me?"

71. Name Your Inner Critic

Giving your inner critic a name will distance you from them so you can look at these thoughts objectively.

Inner Critic Worksheet

Name:

Date:

The Inner Critic is the Voice of Self Doubt

Ways to Recognize Your Inner Critic:

1. Voice critiques you harshly.

2. You feel out of control of this voice. More like you hear it then you create it.

3. It repeats itself over and over (broken record).

4. You know the thought is untrue but it doesn't leave you.

5. It attacks you for hosting the thoughts it just put in your head ie: "Don't be so insecure."

6. It has black and white thinking.

7. It makes arguments that are in your best interest to keep you safe. It often echoes people in your life who are outer critics.

8. It tells us that we are not ready yet (Need to do more work, need for education).

9. It tells us what we are not good at (ie: "You are not good at numbers, technology or public speaking").

1. Getting to Know Your Inner Critic

• What does your critic say?
Write down some of your inner critic's most frequently voiced beliefs.

Inner Critic Worksheet

• Who from your current life or past does the inner critic echo or build upon when it speaks?
Family members, old teachers, cultural messages?

• How would you describe your inner critic? Anxious? People-pleasing? Persistent? Pick five words the describe it.

----

2. Create Your Character

Inner Critic Worksheet

3. Name your Character:

_____

_____

_____

_____

_____

Ways to Distinguish Inner Critic From Realistic Thinking

Inner Critic	Realistic Thinking
Definite pronouncements	Curious questions
Black and White	Able to see the gray
Repetitive	Forward-thinking
Emotionally charged	Emotionally grounded
No interest in actual evidence	Interested in gathering info
Retreat	Explore
Focus on problems/lacking areas	Seeks solutions
Anxious tone	Calmer tone
Self-critique	Self-care

Inner Critic Worksheet

Ways to Work with Your Inner Critic

1. Naming — label and notice

2. Removing from the scene

3. Compassionate understanding of the critic's motives

4. Thanks, but no thanks

5. Separate the I from the Inner Critic

6. Create a character that personifies your inner critic

7. Humor

8. Turn down the volume

9. Move the voice (picture the voice receding into space)

10. Thanks but I got this one covered. *******

72. Recognize Thought Distortion
Challenge the thoughts that affect your self-esteem with this exercise.

Thought Distortion Monitoring Record

Situation	Automatic thought	Emotions & body sensations	Unhelpful thinking style
Who were you with? What were you doing? Where were you? When did it happen?	What went through your mind? (Thoughts, images, or memories)	What did you feel? (Rate intensity 0 - 100%)	Does your thought fall in to any of these common traps?
			☐ **ALL OR NOTHING THINKING** Thinking in extremes. For example, something is either 100% good or bad
			☐ **CATASTROPHIZING** Jumping to the worst possible conclusion
			☐ **OVER GENERALIZING** Seeing a pattern based upon a single event
			☐ **MENTAL FILTER** Only paying attention to certain types of evidence ("that doesn't count")
			☐ **DISQUALIFYING THE POSITIVE** Discounting positive information or twisting a positive into a negative
			☐ **JUMPING TO CONCLUSIONS** Mind reading or predicting the future
			☐ **MINIMIZATION** Discounting the importance of something
			☐ **EMOTIONAL REASONING** Assuming that because we feel a certain way our hunch must be true
			☐ **DEMANDS** Using words like 'should', 'must', and 'ought'
			☐ **LABELLING** Assigning labels to ourselves or others ("I'm rubbish")
			☐ **PERSONALIZATION** Taking too much or too little responsibility
			☐ **LOW FRUSTRATION TOLERANCE** Saying things like "this is too difficult", "this is unbearable" or "I can't stand it"

73. Love Letter

Write a love letter to yourself.

74. Remind Yourself of Your Strengths

Remind yourself of how awesome you are by filling out this worksheet.

My Strengths and Qualities

Things I am good at...
1.
2.
3.

Compliments I have received...
1.
2.
3.

What I like about my appearance...
1.
2.
3.

Challenges I have overcome...
1.
2.
3.

I have helped others by...
1.
2.
3.

Things that make me unique...
1.
2.
3.

What I value the most...
1.
2.
3.

Times I have made others happy...
1.
2.
3.

75. Story of Your Life

Write three stories about yourself by following the instructions in the worksheet.

LIFE STORY

The Past, Present, and Future

Writing a story about your life can help you find meaning and value in your experiences. It will allow you to organize your thoughts and use them to grow. People who develop stories about their life tend to experience a greater sense of meaning, which can contribute to happiness.

The Past

Write the story of your past. Be sure to describe challenges you've overcome, and the personal strengths that allowed you to do so.

LIFE STORY

The Past, Present, and Future

The Present
Describe your life and who you are now. How do you differ from your past self? What are your strengths now? What challenges are you facing?

LIFE STORY

The Past, Present, and Future

The Future

Write about your ideal future. How will your life be different than it is now? How will you be different than you are now?

76. Gratitude Journal

Remind yourself of all the amazing things you have in your life by writing three things you are grateful for every day.

GRATITUDE JOURNAL

Three Good Things

DAY 1

One good thing that happened to me today...

Something good that I saw someone do...

Today I had fun when...

DAY 2

Something I accomplished today...

Something funny that happened today...

Someone I was thankful for today...

GRATITUDE JOURNAL

Three Good Things

DAY 3

Something I was thankful for today...

Today I smiled when...

Something about today I'll always want to remember...

DAY 4

One good thing that happened to me today...

Today was special because...

Today I was proud of myself because...

GRATITUDE JOURNAL

Three Good Things

DAY 5

Something interesting that happened today...

Someone I was thankful for today...

Today I had fun when...

DAY 6

Something about today I'll always want to remember...

Something funny that happened today...

My favorite part of today...

GRATITUDE JOURNAL

Three Good Things

DAY 7

Something I was happy about today...

Something good I saw someone do today...

Something I did well today...

77. Set Life-Enhancing Goals

Set weekly goals to improve your life, like exercising, studying harder, spending less time on social media, or eating healthy.

Setting Goals

_____'s Goal Sheet

This week, my goal is to:
_____
_____
_____

Monday	Tuesday	Wednesday	Thursday	Friday	Saturday	Sunday

78. Forgive Yourself

Forgive yourself for all your past mistakes and things you feel guilty about that are affecting your self-esteem. Write down the things you blame yourself for; take time to forgive yourself for each one, promising never to think about them again.

79. Affirmations

- *I celebrate my uniqueness.*
- *I am beautiful on the inside and outside.*
- *I am perfect and will continue improving and growing.*
- *I accept every part of me.*
- *I am becoming the best version of myself.*

Section 9: No More "Shoulds"

Societal expectations, peer pressure, and rules you force on yourself shape your thoughts, choices, and behaviors. Most of the time, you do what you "should" rather than what you want to do.

Peer pressure may force you to change your behavior.
https://unsplash.com/photos/QozzJpFZ2lg?utm_source=unsplash&utm_medium=referral&utm_content=creditShareLink

"Should" statements are strict rules that dictate how you should behave, act, and live. These thoughts put you under a lot of pressure as you feel you must act in a certain way. You will feel guilty and ashamed if you fail to follow these rules. You have probably caught yourself saying, "I should work out more" or "I should lose weight."

"Should" statements change how you think and become a part of your identity. You don't often realize the effect these thoughts have. When you put unreasonable and unrealistic demands on yourself, you will feel anxious, angry, and sad and will struggle to achieve your goals.

Exercises

80. Why?

"Should" statements have become your natural reaction, so much so that you don't even think about them. Challenge these thoughts by asking, "Why?" This will lead you to explore and identify their authentic values. In other words, you will discover if these thoughts make any difference in your life or if you are just following these rules because you "Should."

Should Statements

Why

Do you need these thoughts in your life?

81. Set Realistic Goals

After identifying the "Should" rules that match your values, change them to goals to relieve the pressure off yourself. For example, turn "I should lose weight" to "My goal is to lose weight and be healthy."

Should Statements/Values

_____

_____

_____

_____

My Goals

_____

_____

_____

_____

82. Rephrase Should Statements

Rephrasing "Should" statements changes how you feel about these thoughts and won't make you feel guilty if you can't achieve them. For example, turn "I shouldn't spend so much time on social media" to "I would like to spend less time on social media."

Should Statements

New Thoughts

----

83. Remove "Should"

Remove the word "Should" from the thought to get to the root of your true feelings. For instance, "I shouldn't feel hurt by what they said" will become "I feel hurt by what they said." See the difference?

Statements With Should

Statements Without Should

----

84. Explore Your Feelings

You may struggle with letting go of "Should" statements. So explore how they make you feel to understand their effect on your mental and emotional health.

Should Statements

_____
_____
_____

How They Make Me Feel

_____
_____
_____

85. Repeat the Thoughts

Write down the "Should" statements, then stand in front of a mirror and repeat them to yourself using "You" instead of "I" or "me." You will realize how damaging these statements are to your self-esteem and that you have been hard on yourself.

86. Meditation

Instructions:
1. Stand under the shower and set the water to a warm temperature.
2. Choose a shower gel scent that relaxes your senses.
3. Feel the water on your skin and every part of your body.
4. Whenever you have an intrusive thought, visualize it going down the drain.
5. Only focus on the present moment and what you are doing, and allow yourself to relax.

87. 4-7-8 Breathing Exercise

Instructions:

1. Place the tip of your tongue behind your upper teeth.
2. Breathe out through your mouth and make a "whoosh" sound.
3. Close your mouth and take a deep breath through your nostrils while counting to four.
4. Hold your breath while counting to seven.
5. Breathe out through your mouth while counting to eight.

88. Write a Letter to Your Future Self

Write a letter to your future self, expressing your life when you lived by "Should" statements and what you hope it will be like when you abandon these thoughts. Read this letter whenever these thoughts creep into your head.

89. Affirmations

- *I live by my own values.*
- *I won't let anyone dictate my thoughts.*
- *I choose a life that makes me happy.*
- *I won't let society's rules influence my thoughts.*
- *I am free to live my life by my own rules.*

Section 10: Peace Within You

It is believed that each person has inner peace. A lot of noise around you can stress you out or cause you anxiety. You need to find your inner peace and use it to silence the negative thoughts in your head.

Finding your inner peace can quiet the negative thoughts in your head.
https://unsplash.com/photos/long-exposure-photography-of-trees-1XGlbRjt92Q

Benefits of Inner Peace and Emotional Balance

- Reduces your stress
- Makes you appreciate the present and be happy
- You avoid bad habits
- You focus on your goals
- Improves your focus
- Gives you power and inner strength
- The ability to recover from setbacks
- Having strong relationships

Mindfulness

You can achieve inner peace by practicing mindful exercises like meditation or breathing exercises. Mindfulness is being present in the here and now and fully aware of your surroundings, your emotions, and what you are doing. This ability protects you from being overwhelmed in any situation and teaches you to react calmly rather than being overwhelmed by your emotions. It is an effective tool against stress and anxiety.

Exercises

90. Reflection Questions

Think hard before answering these questions.

1. If you could change one thing about your life, what would it be and why?

_____
_____
_____

2. If you had the power to travel to the future, ask yourself one question: where/when would it be and why?

_____
_____
_____

3. Think back to the time when you were happiest; what made these days special and why?

___

___

___

91. Mindful Breathing
Instructions:
1. Spread your fingers so your hand looks like a star.
2. Slowly trace your hand's outline using your other hand's pointer finger.
3. Take a deep breath while tracing up from your wrist's tip to your thumb's tip.
4. Breathe out while tracing down the other side of your thumb.
5. Repeat one more time on the same hand and then twice on the other.

92. Mindful Breathing #2
Instructions:
1. Spread out your palm and imagine your hand is a birthday cake and each finger is a candle.
2. Take a deep breath and slowly exhale to blow out each candle.
3. Lower your fingers when you are done, then repeat on the other hand.

93. Body Scan
Instructions:
1. Lie down and close your eyes.
2. Take slow and deep breaths from your belly.
3. Next, bring your attention to your feet and notice how it feels.
4. Notice if you experience any thoughts or emotions, and breathe through them.
5. If you experience any uncomfortable sensation, breathe into it and notice if it changes.
6. Visualize the tension releasing from your body and then disappearing.
7. Repeat with every part of your body.

94. Self-Care Techniques
- Sleep well
- Eat healthily
- Stay hydrated
- Avoid stress and its triggers
- Relax by doing something you enjoy, like watching TV or listening to music
- Get active by dancing and going for walks
- Limit the time you spend on social media

- Get out of the house and spend time with your friends
- Get creative by drawing or writing
- Treat yourself by eating a nice meal or dessert

95. Mindful Eating

Instructions:
1. Grab a piece of your favorite fruit or vegetable.
2. Plan to eat the food while only focusing on the activity of eating and nothing else.
3. Observe the food's shape and color, and notice how it feels in your hand.
4. Take a bite and notice how your mouth moves.
5. Pay attention to the flavor and describe it to yourself.
6. Swallow and feel the aftertaste.
7. Repeat until you finish eating.

96. Yoga

Practice the yoga pose in this illustration and remain in this position for a couple of minutes.

97. Mindful Stretching

Practice the side-to-side neck stretch by pulling your head with one hand from each side, like in the illustration.

98. Connect to Your Senses

Instructions:

1. Look around the room and name five objects you see.
2. Then, name four objects you can touch.
3. Name three sounds you can hear.
4. Name two scents you can smell.
5. Finally, name one thing you can taste.

99. Affirmations

- *I am at peace with the person I have become.*
- *I am surrounded by harmony and peace.*
- *I am connecting to my inner peace.*
- *Peace follows me wherever I go.*
- *Every part of me attracts joy and peace.*

Mindfulness Tracking Sheet

Practice Log

Instruction: Each time you do a formal throughout the weeks of this program, fill out the following log. As you fill it out, and as you look back over the previous week's practice, think about how your practice has been going. Do you notice any patterns about what works best for you? What changes could you make to sustain the discipline? There is an example to show you how to do this.

Date and Formal Practice	Time	Informal Practice	Thoughts, feelings, and sensations that arose during practice and how you felt afterward
12/21 Breathing Space	8 a.m.	Brushing Teeth	My mind kept wandering to all the work I had to do today. I noticed a tightening in my chest at times, but it subsided. That tightness in my chest was anxiousness, and I felt more calm after the practice. For the informal, I never really noticed the sensations of the bristles on my gums, interesting.

Mindfulness Tracking Sheet

Date and Formal Practice	Time	Informal Practice	Thoughts, feelings, and sensations that arose during practice and how you felt afterward

Bonus Section: My Behavior Log

Activity 101

Record in this worksheet all the times you felt anxious during the day, and answer the questions at the end. Print this log to keep track of your anxiety for as long as you need.

 # THOUGHT RECORD

A thought record is helpful for keeping track of your anxiety thoughts throughout the week. Whenever those thoughts come up, make sure to write them down here. Make an effort to change your anxiety thoughts into positive ones and see what happens!

What happened? (Trigger)	How did it make me feel?	Anxiety thoughts that I had	New positive thoughts I tried	What happened? (Outcome)

Then, answer these questions.
1. Does making a behavioral log make you more or less anxious? Why?
2. What was it like to pay attention to your feelings of anxiety by keeping this log?
3. Were you aware that you had many anxiety-related thoughts?
4. What do you want to do to overcome your anxiety?

Thank You

You did it! You finished the book and took a real and powerful step to improve your life. There is no denying that being a teenager has its challenges, but you made the healthy choice to equip yourself with the right tools to get through this stage.

Anxiety, anger, negative thoughts, and fears aren't easy to live with. They can seriously affect your mood, personality, and well-being. CBT can transform your life and put you in control of your emotions rather than have them control you. You will be impressed with how you react to different situations and your ability to handle them.

Thank you for trusting this book and going on this journey!

Check out another book in the series

References

(N.d.). Gov.au. https://www.cci.health.wa.gov.au/-/media/CCI/Consumer-Modules/Back-from-The-Bluez/Back-from-the-Bluez---04---The-ABC-Analysis.pdf

Aid, T. (2019, May 28). Using imagery in CBT. Therapist Aid. https://www.therapistaid.com/therapy-guide/using-imagery-in-cbt

Anxiety and fear in children. (n.d.). Gov.au. https://www.betterhealth.vic.gov.au/health/conditionsandtreatments/fear-and-anxiety-children

Elaine Houston, B. S. (2019, June 17). CBT for children: A guide for helping kids in therapy. Positivepsychology.com. https://positivepsychology.com/cbt-for-children/

Halder, S., & Mahato, A. K. (2019). Cognitive behavior therapy for children and adolescents: Challenges and gaps in practice. Indian Journal of Psychological Medicine, 41(3), 279–283. https://doi.org/10.4103/ijpsym.ijpsym_470_18

Hirschlag, A. (2018, December 18). How to cope with anxiety: 13 simple tips. Healthline. https://www.healthline.com/health/mental-health/how-to-cope-with-anxiety

Nunez, K. (2020, April 17). ABC model of cognitive behavioral therapy: How it works. Healthline. https://www.healthline.com/health/abc-model

Rodriguez, J. (2019, April 10). How journaling benefits your child. Scholastic.com; Scholastic Parents. https://www.scholastic.com/parents/books-and-reading/raise-a-reader-blog/how-journaling-benefits-your-child.html

Ruini, C., & Mortara, C. C. (2022). Writing technique across psychotherapies—from traditional expressive writing to new positive psychology interventions: A narrative review. Journal of Contemporary Psychotherapy, 52(1), 23–34. https://doi.org/10.1007/s10879-021-09520-9

Walter, I. R. (2017, October 10). 10 therapist (and child)-approved activities to support kids with anxiety —. Family Therapy Basics. https://familytherapybasics.com/blog/2017/10/8/10-therapist-and-child-approved-activities-to-support-kids-with-anxiety

(ma), V. S., & (PhD), C. D. (2023, May 14). Mental filtering: Definition and examples. Helpful Professor. https://helpfulprofessor.com/mental-filtering/

(N.d.-a). Org.uk. https://www.mind.org.uk/information-support/drugs-and-treatments/talking-therapy-and-counselling/cognitive-behavioural-therapy-cbt/

(N.d.-b). Choosingtherapy.com. https://www.choosingtherapy.com/cbt-kids-teens/

(N.d.-c). Iscainfo.com. https://iscainfo.com/resources/Documents/CBT%20for%20Teens.pdf

(N.d.-d). Washington.edu. https://depts.washington.edu/uwhatc/wp-content/uploads/2022/07/Cognitive-Triangle_Worksheet_Coping_and_Processing.pdf

(N.d.-e). Therapistaid.com. https://www.therapistaid.com/worksheets/automatic-thoughts

(N.d.-f). Org.uk. https://www.mind.org.uk/information-support/types-of-mental-health-problems/anxiety-and-panic-attacks/causes/

(N.d.-g). Choosingtherapy.com. https://www.choosingtherapy.com/cbt-for-anxiety/

(N.d.-h). Therapistaid.com. https://www.therapistaid.com/worksheets/abc-model-for-rebt

(N.d.-i). Org.uk. https://www.mind.org.uk/information-support/types-of-mental-health-problems/anger/causes-of-anger/

(N.d.-j). Choosingtherapy.com. https://www.choosingtherapy.com/cbt-for-anger/#:~:text=CBT%20for%20anger%20can%20assist,rational%2C%20self%2Dcompassionate%20thoughts.

(N.d.-k). Therapistaid.com. https://www.therapistaid.com/worksheets/behavioral-experiment

(N.d.-l). Therapistaid.com. https://www.therapistaid.com/worksheets/anger-diary

(N.d.-m). Psycom.net. https://www.psycom.net/depression-test

(N.d.-n). Choosingtherapy.com. https://www.choosingtherapy.com/cbt-for-depression/

(N.d.-o). Org.uk. https://www.mind.org.uk/information-support/types-of-mental-health-problems/self-esteem/about-self-esteem/

15 core CBT techniques you can use right now. (2019, July 9). Mark Tyrrell's Therapy Skills; Mark Tyrrell. https://www.unk.com/blog/15-core-cbt-techniques-you-can-use-right-now/

3 instantly calming CBT techniques for anxiety. (2016, March 8). Mark Tyrrell's Therapy Skills; Mark Tyrrell. https://www.unk.com/blog/3-instantly-calming-cbt-techniques-for-anxiety/

50 ways to start practicing self-care. (2016, July 21). International Bipolar Foundation. https://ibpf.org/articles/50-ways-to-start-practicing-self-care/

99 self-love affirmations to use when you're feeling insecure & self-critical. (2023, February 20). Mindbodygreen. https://www.mindbodygreen.com/articles/self-love-affirmations

Albert Bonfil, P. (2022, August 12). Cognitive distortions: Overgeneralizing –. Cognitive Behavioral Therapy Los Angeles. https://cogbtherapy.com/cbt-blog/cognitive-distortions-overgeneralizing

Andrews, W. (2021, May 10). Unhealthy thinking patterns: Should statements ». Design.org. https://design.org/unhealthy-thinking-patterns-should-statements/

Anger - how it affects people. (n.d.). Gov.au. https://www.betterhealth.vic.gov.au/health/healthyliving/anger-how-it-affects-people

Ankrom, S. (2008, June 15). 9 breathing exercises to relieve anxiety. Verywell Mind. https://www.verywellmind.com/abdominal-breathing-2584115

Anxiety disorders. (2018, May 4). Mayo Clinic. https://www.mayoclinic.org/diseases-conditions/anxiety/symptoms-causes/syc-20350961

Anxiety disorders. (n.d.). Cleveland Clinic. https://my.clevelandclinic.org/health/diseases/9536-anxiety-disorders

Arlin Cuncic, M. A. (2010, August 31). What Is Overgeneralization? Verywell Mind. https://www.verywellmind.com/overgeneralization-3024614

Automatic thoughts. (n.d.). Therapist Aid. https://www.therapistaid.com/therapy-worksheet/automatic-thoughts

Behavioral experiment. (n.d.). Therapist Aid. https://www.therapistaid.com/therapy-worksheet/behavioral-experiment/cbt/none

Brady, K. (2020, August 19). 5 ways to stop catastrophizing. Keir Brady Counseling Services. https://keirbradycounseling.com/catastrophizing/

Breathing exercises (deep breathing) to reduce anxiety & depression. (n.d.). https://restorativestrength.com/breathing-exercises-for-anxiety-and-depression/

By, P. (n.d.). List of Emotions. Therapistaid.com. https://www.therapistaid.com/worksheets/list-of-emotions

Carol. (2022, April 30). Mental filtering: What to know about this cognitive distortion. A Cognitive Connection. https://acognitiveconnection.com/cognitive-distortion-mental-filtering/

Casabianca, S. S., & Shatzman, C. (2022, April 25). Positive affirmations for anxiety: Reframing your worry to calm down. Psych Central. https://psychcentral.com/anxiety/affirmations-for-anxiety

CCPS. (2015, February 16). 7 benefits of Cognitive Behavioral Therapy. Comprehensive Consultation Psychological Services. https://comprehendthemind.com/7-benefits-cognitive-behavioral-therapy/

Challenging anxious thoughts. (n.d.). Therapistaid.com. https://www.therapistaid.com/worksheets/challenging-anxious-thoughts

Clinic, A. R. (2020, October 26). The goals of cognitive behavioral therapy? Aquila Recovery Clinic; Aquila Recovery. https://www.aquilarecovery.com/blog/what-are-the-goals-of-cognitive-behavioral-therapy/

Coffey, C. (2018, October 2). 30 Affirmations To Stop Comparing And Celebrate You. Thecoffeybreak.com. https://www.thecoffeybreak.com/blog-2/2018/10/2/30-affirmations-to-stop-comparing-and-celebrate-you

Cognitive restructuring: Decatastrophizing. (n.d.). Therapist Aid. https://www.therapistaid.com/therapy-worksheet/decatastrophizing/cbt/none

Content, M. (n.d.). Journaling: Using 4 Cognitive behavioural therapy exercises. Mossery.

Core beliefs info sheet. (n.d.). Therapist Aid. https://www.therapistaid.com/therapy-worksheet/core-beliefs-info-sheet/cbt/adolescents

Counselling Matters. (2020, October 12). Anger management-understanding triggers-. Counselling Matters. https://counselling-matters.org.uk/anger-management-understanding-triggers/

Courtney E. Ackerman, M. A. (2017a, March 20). CBT techniques: 25 cognitive behavioral therapy worksheets. Positivepsychology.com. https://positivepsychology.com/cbt-cognitive-behavioral-therapy-techniques-worksheets/

Courtney E. Ackerman, M. A. (2017b, September 29). Cognitive distortions: 22 examples & worksheets (& PDF). Positivepsychology.com. https://positivepsychology.com/cognitive-distortions/

Courtney E. Ackerman, M. A. (2018, July 12). What is self-acceptance? 25 exercises + definition & quotes. Positivepsychology.com. https://positivepsychology.com/self-acceptance/

Cundiff, D. (2022, December 19). Benefits of cognitive behavioral therapy. Bayview Recovery Rehab Center. https://www.bayviewrecovery.com/rehab-blog/5-benefits-of-cognitive-behavioral-therapy/

Decatastrophizing. (2023, February 21). Psychology Tools. https://www.psychologytools.com/resource/decatastrophizing/

Department of Health, & Human Services. (n.d.). Depression explained. Gov.au. https://www.betterhealth.vic.gov.au/health/conditionsandtreatments/depression

Deschene, L. (2020, May 14). 8 quick and easy meditation techniques to calm your anxious mind. Tiny Buddha. https://tinybuddha.com/blog/mindfulness-peace-blog/8-quick-and-easy-meditation-techniques-to-calm-your-anxious-mind/

Distinguish between fear and worry. (n.d.). Gdba.com. https://gdba.com/distinguish-between-fear-and-worry/

Driscoll, L. (2020, September 20). 7 CBT activities you can use in school counseling. Social Emotional Workshop. https://www.socialemotionalworkshop.com/cbt-activities-school-counseling/

Dysfunctional Thought Record. (n.d.). B-cdn.net. https://positive.b-cdn.net/wp-content/uploads/2017/06/Dysfunctional-Thought-Record.pdf

Elizabeth, D. (2022, August 4). 53 affirmations for rest and relaxation. Wild Simple Joy. https://wildsimplejoy.com/affirmations-for-rest-and-relaxation/

Emma McAdam, L. (2021, May 22). Mental Filtering: Thinking this way might make you depressed. Therapy in a Nutshell. https://therapyinanutshell.com/mental-filtering/

Emotional balance —. (n.d.). Alternative Health Care Center. http://www.alternativehealthcaredoc.com/emotional-balance

Eskin, C. K. (2021, December 22). Why teens don't talk to their parents. Teen Line. https://www.teenline.org/post/why-teens-don-t-talk-to-their-parents

Example Sheet. (n.d.). The Cognitive Model. Therapistaid.com. https://www.therapistaid.com/worksheets/cognitive-model-example-practice

Facing Your Fears (CYP). (2023, February 21). Psychology Tools. https://www.psychologytools.com/resource/facing-your-fears-cyp/

Felman, A. (2020, January 11). Anxiety: Symptoms, types, causes, prevention, and treatment. Medicalnewstoday.com. https://www.medicalnewstoday.com/articles/323454

Find your inner peace: techniques and benefits. (n.d.). Beaire.com. https://beaire.com/en/aire-magazine/find-your-inner-peace

Fritscher, L. (2008, March 15). The psychology of fear. Verywell Mind. https://www.verywellmind.com/the-psychology-of-fear-2671696

Gillette, H. (2010, March 4). Why are teens depressed? 6 reasons. Psych Central. https://psychcentral.com/depression/why-are-so-many-teens-depressed

GoodRx - error. (n.d.). Goodrx.com. https://www.goodrx.com/health-topic/mental-health/fear-vs-phobia

Gower, B. S., & Stokes, M. C. (Eds.). (2020). Socratic Questions: New Essays on the Philosophy of Socrates and its Significance. Routledge.

Hadiah. (2023, June 12). Top 10 practical CBT exercises for anxiety relief (+FREE worksheets PDF). Ineffable Living; Hadiah. https://ineffableliving.com/treat-your-anxiety-using-cognitive-behavioral-therapy-cbt/

Harrison, P. (2018, February 18). 19 mindfulness-Based Cognitive Behavioral Therapy exercises [CBT]. The Daily Meditation Coaching Sessions; The Daily Meditation. https://www.thedailymeditation.com/cbt-exercises

Harrison, P. (2019, August 22). 4 mindful eating meditation scripts you need to try. The Daily Meditation Coaching Sessions; The Daily Meditation. https://www.thedailymeditation.com/mindful-eating-3

Holland, K., & Nave, K. (2013, December 9). Cognitive behavioral therapy for depression. Healthline. https://www.healthline.com/health/depression/cognitive-behavioral-therapy

Holy, L. (2021, March 1). 10 yoga poses for relaxation & calming. Banyanbotanicals.com; Banyan Botanicals. https://www.banyanbotanicals.com/info/blog-the-banyan-insight/details/10-yoga-poses-for-relaxation-anxiety/

How I Feel. (n.d.). Therapist Aid. https://www.therapistaid.com/therapy-worksheet/how-i-feel-cbt-tool/cbt/adolescents

Kapoor, A. (2021, July 27). How to do Body Scan Meditation and its benefits. Calm Sage. https://www.calmsage.com/mindfulness-body-scan-meditation/

Kendra Cherry, M. (2009, March 3). What is cognitive behavioral therapy (CBT)? Verywell Mind. https://www.verywellmind.com/what-is-cognitive-behavior-therapy-2795747

Kendra Cherry, M. (2013, August 2). Emotions and types of emotional responses. Verywell Mind. https://www.verywellmind.com/what-are-emotions-2795178

Kristenson, S. (2022, April 12). 60 calming affirmations for managing your anger. Happier Human; Steve Scott. https://www.happierhuman.com/affirmations-anger/

Kristenson, S. (2023, July 10). 60 affirmations for a calming peace of mind. Happier Human; Steve Scott. https://www.happierhuman.com/affirmations-peace/

LaBarbara, S. (2022, August 25). The trouble with 'should statements' and how to reframe them. A Good Place. https://www.agoodplacetherapy.com/the-blog/should-statements

Lamoreux, K. (2016, January 24). 1-minute mindfulness exercises. Psych Central. https://psychcentral.com/health/minute-mindfulness-exercises

Lautieri, A. (2019, March 13). Visualization and guided imagery techniques for stress reduction. Mentalhelp.net; admin. https://www.mentalhelp.net/stress/visualization-and-guided-imagery-techniques-for-stress-reduction/

Leavitt, B. (2018, March 6). Shoulds and shouldy thinking. Bill Leavitt Therapist; Bill Leavitt Counseling & Therapy. https://billleavitttherapy.com/shoulds-shouldy-thinking/

Levitt, S. (2023, March 1). What is the difference between a fear and a phobia? Pathways; Pathways Counseling Services. https://www.pathwayscounselingsvcs.com/what-is-the-difference-between-a-fear-and-a-phobia/

Lovering, C. (2016, May 17). 7 best relaxation exercises: Meditation, grounding, and more. Psych Central. https://psychcentral.com/lib/relaxation-exercises-and-techniques

Lukin, K. (2016, September 8). Cognitive behavioral therapy exercises. Lukin Center for Psychotherapy; Lukin Center. https://www.lukincenter.com/5-surprisingly-effective-cognitive-behavioral-therapy-exercises/

Margarita Tartakovsky, M. S. (2016, October 3). Should statements running your life? This might help. Psych Central. https://psychcentral.com/blog/weightless/2016/10/should-statements-running-your-life-this-might-help

May. (2019, May 22). Am I depressed or just sad? Take this quiz to find out. Advantage Care Health Center. https://advantagecaredtc.org/am-i-depressed-or-just-sad/

Mcleod, S., & Evans, O. G. (2022, November 3). Cognitive behavioral therapy (CBT): Types, techniques, uses. Simply Psychology. https://www.simplypsychology.org/cognitive-therapy.html

Millacci, T. S. (2020, October 28). How to relax: Best relaxation techniques for anxiety. Positivepsychology.com. https://positivepsychology.com/relaxation-techniques-anxiety/

Mindful breathing exercises. (2021, March 21). Action for Healthy Kids. https://www.actionforhealthykids.org/activity/mindful-breathing-exercises/

Mooditude. (2021, July 21). Automatic negative thoughts - things you need to know for breaking the habit - mooditude – A happier you! Mooditude – A Happier You! https://mooditude.app/post/automatic-negative-thoughts-things-you-need-to-know-for-breaking-the-habit/

Nicholson, M. (2019, June 5). Safety behaviors. Austin Anxiety Therapists. https://www.austinanxiety.com/safety-behaviors/

Nunez, K. (2020, April 17). ABC model of cognitive behavioral therapy: How it works. Healthline. https://www.healthline.com/health/abc-model

Ohwovoriole, T. (2021, April 13). Understanding Anger. Verywell Mind. https://www.verywellmind.com/what-is-anger-5120208

Perry, E. (n.d.). The purpose of fear and how to overcome it. Betterup.com. https://www.betterup.com/blog/purpose-of-fear

Peterson, A. L. (2019, May 24). What is... A safety behaviour in CBT - mental health @ home. Mental Health @ Home. https://mentalhealthathome.org/2019/05/24/what-is-safety-behaviour/

Pietrangelo, A. (2019, December 12). CBT techniques: Tools for cognitive behavioral therapy. Healthline. https://www.healthline.com/health/cbt-techniques

Positive activities for behavioral activation. (n.d.). Therapist Aid. https://www.therapistaid.com/therapy-worksheet/activities-behavioral-activation/cbt/none

Psychologists, M. (2019, August 12). What are the benefits of cognitive behaviour therapy (CBT)? MyLife Psychologists. https://mylifepsychologists.com.au/what-are-the-benefits-of-cognitive-behaviour-therapy-cbt/

Rabin, P. L. (1983). What is depression? Nephrology Nurse, 5(1), 20-22. https://www.unicef.org/parenting/mental-health/what-is-depression?gclid=CjwKCAjwq4imBhBQEiwA9Nx1BrzSshzQ6LVvMmjM1CfnW2wbY9chnLOeO97HnRR8K1vDD7Ae9YHxPRoCXAQQAvD_BwE

Rachel. (2020, April 21). Black and white thinking: 9 easy ways to stop for good - planning mindfully. Planning Mindfully - Designing Life with Intention. https://www.planningmindfully.com/black-and-white-thinking/

Remez, S. (2021, January 9). 11 benefits of peace of mind and being tranquil. Success Consciousness | Positive Thinking - Personal Development. https://www.successconsciousness.com/blog/inner-peace/benefits-of-peace-of-mind/

Rollo, N. (2019, February 6). Square breathing: How to reduce stress through breathwork. The Couch: A Therapy & Mental Wellness Blog. https://blog.zencare.co/square-breathing/

Roncero, A. (n.d.). Automatic thoughts: How to identify and fix them. Betterup.com. https://www.betterup.com/blog/automatic-thoughts

Self-esteem and teenagers. (n.d.). Reachout.com. https://parents.au.reachout.com/common-concerns/everyday-issues/self-esteem-and-teenagers

Selva, J., & Bc, S. (2018, March 16). Challenging negative automatic thoughts: 5 worksheets (+PDF). Positivepsychology.com. https://positivepsychology.com/challenging-automatic-thoughts-positive-thoughts-worksheets/

Sim, M. (2023, March 9). 25 activities to help your students combat cognitive distortions. Teaching Expertise; dontan. https://www.teachingexpertise.com/classroom-ideas/cognitive-distortions-activity/

Solving problems the cognitive-behavioral way. (n.d.). Psychology Today. https://www.psychologytoday.com/us/blog/all-about-cognitive-and-behavior-therapy/202202/solving-problems-the-cognitive-behavioral-way

Specific phobias. (2023, June 9). Mayo Clinic. https://www.mayoclinic.org/diseases-conditions/specific-phobias/symptoms-causes/syc-20355156

Star, K. (2011, September 13). How "should" statements contribute to panic and anxiety. Verywell Mind. https://www.verywellmind.com/should-statements-2584193

Susan. (2023, January 16). 85 daily affirmations to change your negative thoughts. Sassy Sister Stuff. https://www.sassysisterstuff.com/affirmations-for-negative-thoughts/

Sutton, J. (2020, September 24). 16 decatastrophizing tools, worksheets, and role-plays. Positivepsychology.com. https://positivepsychology.com/decatastrophizing-worksheets/

Sutton, J. (2021, July 24). How to boost self-esteem: 12 simple exercises & CBT tools. Positivepsychology.com. https://positivepsychology.com/self-esteem-boost-exercises/

Teen depression. (2022, August 12). Mayo Clinic. https://www.mayoclinic.org/diseases-conditions/teen-depression/symptoms-causes/syc-20350985

The Depression Project. (2023a, February 10). 75+ positive affirmations for depression. The Depression Project. https://thedepressionproject.com/blogs/news/the-best-positive-affirmations-for-depression

The Depression Project. (2023b, April 5). 3 DBT mindfulness exercises for depression, anxiety & PTSD. The Depression Project. https://thedepressionproject.com/blogs/news/3-dbt-mindfulness-exercises-for-depression-anxiety-ptsd

The difference between fear and phobia. (n.d.). Alliedpsychiatry.com. https://www.alliedpsychiatry.com/blog/the-difference-between-fear-and-phobia

The past, present, and future. (n.d.). Therapistaid.com. https://www.therapistaid.com/worksheets/life-story

The relationship between thoughts, feelings and behaviors. (n.d.). Debbiewoodallcarroll.com. https://debbiewoodallcarroll.com/the-relationship-between-thoughts-feelings-and-behaviors/

Thoughts & behaviors: Costs and benefits. (n.d.). Therapist Aid. https://www.therapistaid.com/therapy-worksheet/cost-benefit-analysis/cbt/adolescents

United We Care. (2023, May 24). The Startling Effects of Anger on Your Mind and Body: Learn more now. United We Care | A Super App for Mental Wellness; United We Care. https://www.unitedwecare.com/the-startling-effects-of-anger-on-your-mind-and-body-learn-more-now/

Using Thought Records to track & challenge thoughts. (2018, April 10). Psychology Tools. https://www.psychologytools.com/self-help/thought-records/

Vallejo, M. (2022, September 7). Mental filter: A cognitive distortion. Mental Health Center Kids. https://mentalhealthcenterkids.com/blogs/articles/mental-filter

Valls, M. (2019, March 7). 10 journal prompts for self-reflection and inner peace. Bee Happi Vintage Press |; Bee Happi Vintage Press. https://beehappi.com/happiness-and-well-being/10-journal-prompts-for-self-reflection-and-inner-peace/

Wagner, K. D. (2016, April 18). 17 affirmations to release negative thoughts. Spirituality+Health. https://www.spiritualityhealth.com/articles/2016/04/18/17-affirmations-release-negative-thoughts

Ward, L. (2021, December 18). 7 yoga poses to inspire your creative side and practice mindful movement. YouAlignedTM. https://youaligned.com/yoga/mindful-movement-yoga-poses/

Weekly schedule for behavioral activation. (n.d.). Therapist Aid. https://www.therapistaid.com/therapy-worksheet/schedule-behavioral-activation/cbt/none

what are emotions? (2015). In What is this thing called Philosophy? (pp. 183–192). Routledge.

What are the benefits of cognitive behavioral therapy (CBT)? (n.d.). Northstartransitions.com. https://www.northstartransitions.com/post/what-are-the-benefits-of-cognitive-behavioral-therapy-cbt

What is anger? Definition & psychology behind this emotion. (n.d.). Betterhelp.com. https://www.betterhelp.com/advice/anger/what-is-anger-definition-psychology-behind-this-emotion/

What is behaviour? - Principles for effective support. (n.d.). Gov.au. https://www.health.nsw.gov.au/mentalhealth/psychosocial/principles/Pages/behaviour-whatis.aspx

What is fear? (2019, September 17). Paul Ekman Group. https://www.paulekman.com/universal-emotions/what-is-fear/

What is mindfulness? (2020). In Building and Sustaining a Teaching Career (pp. 15–28). Cambridge University Press.

What is the Cognitive Triangle and How is it Used? (2021, September 13). KASA Solutions. https://kasa-solutions.com/what-is-the-cognitive-triangle-and-how-is-it-used/

Williams, A. J. (n.d.). A quote from The Psychic Mind. Goodreads.com. https://www.goodreads.com/quotes/1344024-thoughts-create-emotions-emotions-create-feelings-and-feelings-create-behaviour

Williamson, T. (2021, June 1). 10 breathing exercises for kids with anxiety or anger. Mindfulmazing.com; Mindfulmazing. https://www.mindfulmazing.com/10-breathing-exercises-for-kids-with-anxiety-or-anger/

Wood, K. (2020, November 9). The connection between thoughts and emotions. Kamini Wood. https://www.kaminiwood.com/the-connection-between-thoughts-and-emotions/

Worry exploration questions. (n.d.). Therapist Aid. https://www.therapistaid.com/therapy-worksheet/worry-exploration-questions/cbt/adolescents

Zayed, A. (2022, November 1). 4 Benefits of Cognitive behavioral therapy. The Diamond Rehab Thailand; Theo de Vries. https://diamondrehabthailand.com/cognitive-behavioral-therapy-benefits/

Zorbas, A. (2021, July 30). Should statements: Reframe the way you think. Therapy Now. https://www.therapynowsf.com/blog/should-statements-reframe-the-way-you-think

Carol. (2022, April 30). Mental filtering: What to know about this cognitive distortion. A Cognitive Connection. https://acognitiveconnection.com/cognitive-distortion-mental-filtering/

Rebecca Joy Stanborough, M. F. A. (2020, February 4). Cognitive restructuring: Techniques and examples. Healthline. https://www.healthline.com/health/cognitive-restructuring

(N.d.). Choosingtherapy.com. Retrieved August 20, 2023, from https://www.choosingtherapy.com/cognitive-restructuring/

www.ingramcontent.com/pod-product-compliance
Lightning Source LLC
Chambersburg PA
CBHW060414010526
44107CB00006B/686